D1498429

CREATION
of the
MODERN MIDDLE EAST

United Arab Emirates

CREATION

of the

MODERN MIDDLE EAST

CREATION
of the
MODERN MIDDLE EAST

United Arab Emirates

Susan Muaddi Darraj and Meredyth Puller |
Series Editor: Arthur Goldschmidt Jr.

CHELSEA HOUSE
PUBLISHERS
An imprint of Infobase Publishing

Library of Congress Cataloging-in-Publication Data
Darraj, Susan Muaddi.
 United Arab Emirates / by Susan Muaddi Darraj and Meredyth Puller.
 p. cm. — (Creation of the modern Middle East)
 Includes bibliographical references and index.
 ISBN 978-1-60413-071-3 (hardcover)
 1. United Arab Emirates—Juvenile literature. I. Puller, Meredyth. II. Title.
III. Series.
 DS247.T8D37 2008
 953.57—dc22   2008016786

Series design by Annie O'Donnell
Cover design by Jooyoung An

Printed in the United States of America

Bang EJB 10 9 8 7 6 5 4 3 2 1

This book is printed on acid-free paper.

All links and Web addresses were checked and verified to be correct at the time of publication. Because of the dynamic nature of the Web, some addresses and links may have changed since publication and may no longer be valid.

Contents

A New World Wonder

In history classes, students are sometimes quizzed about the seven "Wonders of the Ancient World," the term used to categorize the Great Pyramids at Giza, the Colossus of Rhodes, the Lighthouse of Alexandria, the Hanging Gardens of Babylon, the Statue of Zeus at Olympia, the Temple of Artemis at Ephesus, and the Mausoleum of Halicarnassus. There are also other lists of Wonders, which include the Wonders of the Middle Ages: this list includes the Great Wall of China, the Taj Mahal, and other amazing and awe-inspiring man-made structures.

In the future, however, there may be another item to add to that list: The Palm Islands of Dubai, one of the seven members of the United Arab Emirates (UAE).

It is truly startling to comprehend the scope of this project: the emirate of Dubai has plans underway to build the three largest man-made islands in the world off the coast of the UAE. The three islands, Palm Jumeirah, Palm Diera, and Palm Jebel Ali, will—when seen from the air—each be shaped like a date palm tree. Its land masses will be formed into a tree trunk that extends out from the Dubai coast, topped with palm fronds, and several islands in a semi-circle around it as a breakwater to protect it from the tides.

Three islands, each like a giant palm tree—together, they will extend the coast line of Dubai by seventy-two miles and, according to the emirates plans, make the UAE the undisputed leader in international tourism.

One of the newest modern marvels in the world, the man-made islands of Dubai in the United Arab Emirates extends from the shoreline to form a palm date tree. The first completed island, the Palm Jumeirah, features luxurious housing, fancy hotel accommodations, a monorail, and a sub-sea tunnel. The other two islands, Palm Diera and Palm Jebel Ali *(above, in model form)*, are still under construction.

SEVEN TINY KINGDOMS

The emirates, called such because they are governed or owned by "emirs" (Arabic for "princes") or sheikhs—the rulers of each tribal region—are located along what is called the Coast of Oman. The Arabian Peninsula, which juts out into the Persian Gulf, is mostly composed of Saudi Arabia, a country that is home to the two holiest cities in Islam: Mecca and Medina. On the southern coast of the peninsula is the country of Oman. Along a curve to the northern edge lie the seven tiny emirates: Dubai, Abu Dhabi, Sharjah, Ras al-Khaimah, Ajman, Umm al-Qaiwan, and Fujairah. Despite their size, their location is strategic because they sit at the point that is the narrow entrance to the Gulf.

While four-fifths of the landmass on the peninsula is desert and barren, the coastline of the emirates is dotted with specks of small islands and beautiful coral reefs. The seasons do not vary much in the emirates, as the temperature is usually warm, reaching as high as 75 degrees Fahrenheit even in the winter months. The climate is tropical, which means that the heat is accompanied by high levels of humidity.

Their history as independent states is still very young, but their history as individual Arabian tribes is much older. The emirates were villages, inhabited for thousands of years by inhabitants who lived off fishing and small-scale agriculture. They originated in the Arabian Peninsula, and were of two distinct Arabian tribes: the Yemeni tribes (known today as the Hinnawi) who originated in the southern part of the peninsula and the Nizar tribes (known as the Ghafiri), who hailed from the northern part. Today, people still see themselves as descendants of either the Hinnawi or the Ghafiri, but over the centuries the two have probably blended together to some extent. More people continued to migrate to the coast, for different reasons. One story claims that a dam in the southern part of the Arabian Peninsula broke, between A.D. 100 and 200, causing its inhabitants to abandon their homes and move to the shores.

No matter which Arabian tribe they claimed as their ancestors, the people of the coast depended on the sea for their food and their livelihood. Long before the Gulf attracted the attention of the Europeans and Americans for its oil resources, it was one of the most important trade routes in the Eastern Hemisphere. For thousands of years, the body of water offered ships access to Persia, Iraq, India, Africa, and China.

United Arab Emirates

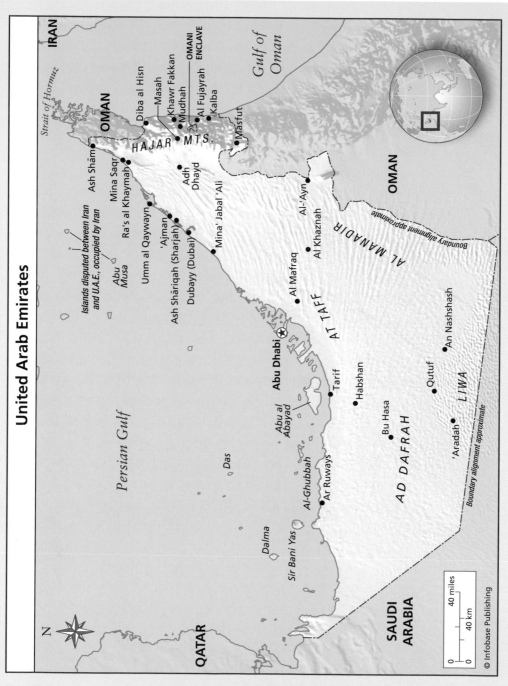

IRAN

Strait of Hormuz

OMAN

Ash Shām

Mina Saqr

Ra's al Khaymah

Islands disputed between Iran
and U.A.E., occupied by Iran

Abu
Musa

Umm al Qaywayn

'Ajman

Ash Shāriqah (Sharjah)

Dubayy (Dubai)

Diba al Hisn

Masah

Khawr Fakkan

Mudhah

Al Fujayrah

Kalba

OMANI
ENCLAVE

Masfut

HAJAR MTS.

Adh
Dhayd

Mina' Jabal 'Ali

Gulf of
Oman

OMAN

Al-'Ayn

Al Khaznah

Al Mafraq

AL MANADIR

Boundary alignment approximate

AT TAFF

Tarif

Habshan

Bu Hasa

AD DAFRAH

An Nashshash

Qutuf

LIWA

'Aradah

Boundary alignment approximate

Abu Dhabi

Abu al
Abayad

Al-Ghubbah

Ar Ruways

Das

Dalma

Sir Bani Yas

Persian Gulf

N

QATAR

SAUDI
ARABIA

40 miles

40 km

0

0

© Infobase Publishing

Bordering Saudi Arabia and Oman, the United Arab Emirates is located on the Persian Gulf. While the country is mostly desert, it does benefit from some mountains in its northwestern region.

The people consisted of two main types: *Hadr*, the towns-people, and *Bedou*, the nomads who travel the deserts. Each was governed by its own sheikh, and each was attuned to its own problems and needs. They saw other tribes and sheikh-doms as rivals and often conducted raids upon and battled one another for territory or gold. Their individual needs would not coalesce until the mid-1960s, and they would not officially unite until 1971.

In the 600s, the people of this region converted to Islam. Before then, many religious traditions co-existed, usually with each tribe or village practicing its own religion. In 622 the Prophet Muhammad entered Medina in the inner Arabian Peninsula, capturing it, uniting the Arabian tribes under the Muslim banner, and establishing Islam as the dominant religion. Before long, most of the region had adopted Islam, including the small fishing villages on the coast. The Sharia, or rules and laws of Islam was adopted by these tribes, which changed the ways in which they lived. For example, a man was permitted four wives, which many scholars agree was actually a limit placed on marriage, not a form of license as some Westerners imagine. Before Islam, men could have wives numbering in the hundreds. The holy book of Islam, the Koran, specifically stated that a man could take up to four wives only if he could provide equally for all of them which, as the Prophet Muhammad stated, most men cannot do. Other laws prescribed severe punishments for murder, theft, falsely accusing another of immoral behavior, and highway robbery.

Several Islamic dynasties governed the Middle East in the centuries after the Prophet Muhammad. One of the greatest eras took place under the rule of the Abbasids, who governed from Iraq. During that era, the arts and culture flourished, as did trade. Because sea transport was cheaper than transporting goods over land, the people of the Gulf region especially benefited from their position on the Gulf waters and played a leading role in the trade conducted between the Muslim world and the Far East. Shipments of precious stones, silks, teas, and other items were highly sought-after in Europe, and the Gulf was the main artery to transport them from India and China. In fact, the stories of Sinbad the Sailor and his adventures became part of the oral tapestry of the *1001 Arabian Nights*, one of the literary highlights of this era. This is just one example of how the economy and culture of the Arabian world was linked to the sea.

Around 1498, the Portuguese, also a skilled seafaring people, arrived in the Arabian Gulf. Vasco da Gama, the renowned Portuguese explorer, set sail in 1497 and sailed around Africa, heading for the Gulf. While he did not actually reach the land inhabited by the United Arab Emirates today, he cleared the way for other Portuguese to trade in the Middle East. Donald Hawley, author of *The Trucial States*, writes, "The trade of the Indian Ocean was then largely in Arab hands." The Portuguese became the dominant force, although, over the next 200 years, many more European nations would compete for mastery in the Gulf, because of its vital role as a trade route to the Far East. Hawley describes a struggle for trade and power in the Gulf in which Portuguese, English, Dutch, French, and Turks all participated, as well as the Arabs and Persians. It was an era of sea battles, fighting between the European powers and landings and attacks from the sea as well as exploitation of the rich trade of the East.

The Arabian Peninsula was and still is the center of the Islamic world. As the Islamic empire expanded, political rule was exercised from places as diverse as modern-day Iraq (the Abbasids) to modern-day Egypt (the Fatimids). The spiritual center, however, always remained Mecca, the birthplace of the Prophet Muhammad.

Living conditions in the peninsula were harsh, and tribes often fought over land and natural resources, especially for things as vital as water. Two major tribes, the Qawasim and the Bani Yas, eventually left the inner Arabian Peninsula and headed for the coast. Their descendants would form the modern-day population of the emirates.

THE QAWASIM:
RAS AL-KHAIMAH AND SHARJAH

The Qawasim (the plural of the family name al-Qasim), an important dynasty, established itself in the early 1700s in the areas known now as Ras al-Khaimah and Sharjah. At the time, both were significant ports, but governed together as one entity. Before they settled in the region, Ras al-Khaimah (which means "the top of the tent" in Arabic) was known as Julfar, a simple port village whose inhabitants lived in simple wooden houses and made a living through fishing.

Ras al-Khaimah currently occupies about 656 square miles. Sharjah, which is located closer to Oman and which comprises over 1000 square miles, is the third largest of the emirates. One of their most important leaders was Sheikh Rashid ibn Mattar bin Rahman al-Qasimi (1727–1777), who claimed to be descended from the Prophet Muhammad. The Qawasim were influenced by Wahhabism, a Muslim movement that swept the peninsula in the 1700s. It was a reform movement, inspired by the man who gave it its name: Muhammad ibn Abd-al-Wahhab. It was called on Muslims to adopt a stricter interpretation of their religion, treating the Koran and the Hadith (the body of authenticated statements about what the Prophet said, did, or approved of in the actions of his associates) as fundamental texts, to be interpreted literally. Journalist Roger Hardy writes, "Like many revivalists in the course of Muslim history, Muhammad Ibn Abd-al-Wahhab, the founder of the movement, felt that the local practice of Islam had lost its original purity." The Wahhabists preached social conservatism and modesty in dress, as well as a separation of women and men in public, and making ritual prayer central to one's daily routine. The modern kingdom of Saudi Arabia is heavily influenced by Wahhabism, as the Wahhabis formed an alliance with the Saud tribe, and helped to establish dominance in the peninsula and to build the Saudi kingdom. By 1800, the Wahhabis also controlled the Trucial Coast. Donald Hawley writes that "Wahhabi religious fervour affected the Qawasim, who were driven by the zeal of the converted to a degree of aggressiveness at sea which they might have otherwise not have attained."

Known as a seafaring clan, the Qawasim in Ras al-Khaimah, their capital, were bold and fearsome. They initiated and conducted pirate raids on British and other ships that sailed the coast. They were in an optimal position to do this, especially since their centers were located on the tip of the curve, at the very point where ships must enter the Gulf. According to Donald Hawley, they had three types of ships, all of which had their special uses and advantages on the waters of the Gulf coast. The vessels of the Qawasim were faster and could be used in shallow waters, and they were easier to maneuver and steer than the heavier European ships. British captain F.E. Loch described their style of pirating: The pirates would target a ship, approach it from the stern side, then pour onto its decks in great numbers, where they engaged in hand-to-hand combat. Their skill and daring easily overwhelmed their victims.

Some estimates say that the Qawasim had more than 800 ships sailing the waters to attack foreign vessels and trading ships. Many believe, however, that they were interested less in piracy and more in becoming involved in the trade route to and from India, which was so profitable to them, as well as to the Europeans.

In 1869, Sharjah and Ras al-Khaimah became two independent entities. Sharjah came to be ruled by another branch of the al-Qasim family, and it would enjoy a deep and vibrant cultural

---

(opposite) During the Spice Trade, all the major European powers were looking to capitalize on business by colonizing spice providers like India and Africa. It was around the 1800s in the Persian Gulf when the Qawasim, a sea-based group of family and friends, took over the local spice trade.

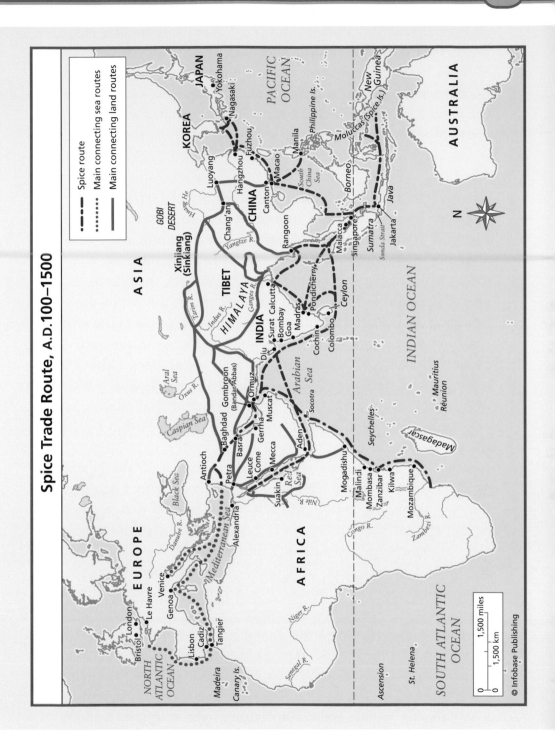

Spice Trade Route, A.D.100–1500

Spice route
Main connecting sea routes
Main connecting land routes

© Infobase Publishing

and intellectual life. In 1871, however, one of its smaller cities ceded from Sharjah. The entity of Kalba was short-lived, however, as it was re-incorporated into Sharjah by 1952. Sharjah became central in Great Britain's plans to exercise control over the region; in 1932, the first airport in the emirates was built in Sharjah by the British government.

THE BANI YAS: DUBAI AND ABU DHABI

The Bani Yas was actually a loose federation of several desert Bedouin tribes, including al-Bufalah, al-Hawamil, al-Mazari, al-Sudan, al-Rimithat, and al-Marar. Its descendants now comprise the ruling families of Dubai and Abu Dhabi, the two largest and richest of the emirates in the federation. In their early days, however, the lives of their citizens were just as humble as those of neighboring villages and tribes. *Abu Dhabi* means "father of the gazelle" in Arabic. The meaning of *Dubai* is less clear, although some sources believe it is derived from the word *daba*, which is a prosperous market, while others contend that *daba* actually means "to creep," as in the slow pace of a creek that marks the landscape.

The Bani Yas settled around the current area of Abu Dhabi in 1761. Their economy was based primarily on camel herding, the traditional occupation of their Bedouin forebears, as well as fishing and pearl diving. In fact, Abu Dhabi had the largest fleet of vessels for pearl diving, numbering 410 (Sharjah had the second largest fleet, at 360 vessels). The sheikhs of Abu Dhabi, as of other sheikhdoms, made money largely by collecting a tax on the pearl-diving vessels.

A revolt against their leader in 1855 swept a new ruler to the tribe's top position: Sheikh Zayed bin Khalifah al-Nahyan, who is commonly referred to by citizens of the UAE as Zayed the Great. Historian Morsy Abdullah describes Sheikh Zayed bin Khalifah as a "gallant warrior by nature," who sought to acquire more land for Abu Dhabi and also unify the tribes of the Bani

Yas. He gained the favor and admiration of many Bedouins when he killed Sheikh Khalid bin Sultan in battle in 1868, resolving a series of disputes with Sharjah and cementing Abu Dhabi's position as the most powerful country in the region. This led many Qawasim leaders to also respect him and seek to make him a friend rather than an enemy. By the late 1800s, Zayed the Great had unified many of the tribes by either warfare or negotiation. His charisma and formidableness made the British government, whose ships sailed the Gulf on the way to its colony in India, nervous.

Dubai was settled in the mid-1700s, but had always been a settlement of sheep- and goat-herders. Its earlier inhabitants also grew date palms: the edible fruit of the date palm tree was a staple of the coastal diet. Dubai had also been a major center of pearl diving for centuries. Records show that divers from Europe even came to Dubai to search for pearls.

Historian Donald Hawley notes that Dubai, the capital city of the emirate, which shares the same name, has been referred to as the "Venice of the Gulf." Just as rivers and canals make the landscape of Venice, Italy, memorable, so too in Dubai: "A wide creek separates the town into two halves," Hawley writes, "and small, gaily painted boats move constantly across the clear, blue-green water."

Dubai was originally established as a sub-set of Abu Dhabi, until it became an independent sheikhdom in 1833 when the al-Makhtoum family—part of the Bani Yas—left Abu Dhabi to assume power in Dubai. Though the Al-Makhtoum family seized control without major obstacles, Dubai and Abu Dhabi became hostile neighbors, always in competition. In 1835 the Abu Dhabi sect of the Bani Yas became briefly involved in piracy, but they were stopped by the British.

By 1903, ships from Great Britain's colony in India began landing regularly in Dubai rather than on the Persian coast, which at the time was still very lawless, an era which historian Morsy Abdullah refers to as "the rise of Dubai." Specifically,

Dubai emerged as a major commercial and trade port, encouraged by its leader's smart business sense. Sheikh Maktum II bin Hushur "had abolished the 5 percent customs duty and declared Dubai a free port," writes Morsy Abdullah. It would eventually become one of the richest of the emirates and the most advanced in terms of commercialism and technology.

Since the time of the ancient leader Hammurabi, slavery had been present in the Middle East region, and continued to provide the basis of labor for several empires until the Civil War in the United States. The spread of Islam in Africa connected the Middle East to the African slave trade *(above)*, leading to the use of African slaves throughout the Persian Gulf and Indian Ocean areas.

AJMAN, UMM AL-QAWAIN, AND FUJAIRAH

Fujairah is unique among the emirates because it is almost completely in a mountainous region, which means that it also has the highest rainfall for the region. The rest of the region, and certainly the other emirates, are mostly desert. Therefore, farming has been more profitable in Fujairah than in its neighboring areas. Al-Fujairah is ruled by the al-Sharqi clan, who split off from the Qawasim of Sharjah around 1866. From that time, various disputes kept it at war with Sharjah's leaders. Fujairah became independent in the early 1900s (although the British did not recognize it until 1952).

Umm al-Qawain has a land mass of 300 square miles. Its name in Arabic means "the mother of two powers." It was founded in 1775 by Sheikh Majid al-Mualla, a member of the al-Ali clan. Donald Hawley writes, "The internal affairs of Umm al-Qawain have been remarkably peaceful and the ruling family are of unusual longevity."

Ajman is the smallest of the emirates, with a total land mass of only 100 square miles. Its leaders tried to resist Wahhabi influence in the early 1800s and even sought British help in preventing its spread to the sheikhdom. It is currently ruled by the al-Nuaimi family.

In their history, Umm al-Qawain, Ajman, and Sharjah were deeply involved in the slave trade, which the British treaties attempted to stop. For example, during the early 1800s, ships carrying slaves from the African coast were intercepted numerous times. Many nations, including the United States, were still actively practicing slavery, so the demand was high. It was not until the 1900s that the trade was completely stopped.

2

The Trucial Coast

It is hard to imagine that the Dubai coast that will soon house approximately 60 luxury hotels and hundreds of multi-million–dollar residences was known a century ago as the Pirate Coast. In fact, the coast of the United Arab Emirates—the federation of Sharjah, Fujairah, Umm al-Qaiwain, Dubai, Abu Dhabi, Ras al-Khaimah, and Ajman—was considered dangerous territory for ships to navigate. The British, who had exercised power in the region for many decades, had a serious problem on their hands because their ships could never travel safely in the Gulf.

India was frequently called the "jewel in the crown" of the British Empire because of its great wealth. Even before India became a British colony, however, the British East India Company had conducted trade with India. The East India Company was solely a trading enterprise until 1688, when it signed an agreement with the British government. This agreement gave the East India Company administrative and military authority over the region. The British government valued the East India Company and the revenues it generated.

Therefore, Great Britain wanted to ensure a safe passage for its merchant ships and military vessels to India, rendering the Persian Gulf, like other routes through the Middle East, important for the British. They did not want other countries to establish naval bases in the Gulf that might impede their free passage to India.

Many of the inhabitants of the coast, mostly of the Qawasim tribe, made their living as pirates, hijacking ships and vessels and stealing their cargos. These pirates conducted their raids despite attempts by the local sheikhs to patrol the coast and protect the vessels from attack. Before long, the coast of these sheikhdoms had come to be known as the Pirate Coast.

Historians point out, however, that it was not only the Arabs who conducted piracy on the Gulf waters. Many Europeans were pirates, such as Captain James Gillam, whose gang attacked and killed Captain Edgecomb, a frigate commander for the British East India Company. He also allegedly convinced his victim's men to become pirates and work with him in attacking and raiding other vessels. In 1700 he was captured, imprisoned, and executed in Great Britain. Donald Hawley writes, "The Europeans . . . joined in the pirateering, menacing the Gulf and Indian Ocean as much as their Arab rivals, and Indian pirates were also active."

By the mid-1700s, the Qawasim had become a stronger force, mainly because they had acquired weapons. Therefore, the Qawasim pirates, who were more numerous, presented a major threat to Great Britain. In 1778, they captured one of its ships and ransomed it for 4,000 rupees; again, in 1797, another British ship was captured, but the sheikh of Ras al-Khaimah ordered it to be released. A few months later, however, a more serious attack occurred on yet another British vessel and British officials were injured.

THE TRUCIAL STATES

Obliged to act decisively, the British destroyed the Qawasim capital, Ras al-Khaimah, in 1819. Their forces raided and seized every major Qawasim stronghold. The British lost several men, but the Qawasim numbers of killed and wounded numbered in the hundreds. During the capture of Ras al-Khaimah alone, the British lost 5 men, while the Qawasim lost almost 400.

The British also opted to work with the local sheikhs to protect their trading vessels. In 1820, the British signed the General Treaty for the Cessation of Plunder and Piracy with the sheikhs of the small villages. According to Donald Hawley, this was "the first treaty to impose an obligation on any part of Arabia." The treaty was negotiated by British representative Captain T. Perronet Thompson, who spoke Arabic and respected the Arabs of the coast. Hawley writes that Thompson even hoped to convert the sheikhs and their tribes to Christianity, but they rejected his attempts. The Arabs, however, were respectful of Christians and even allowed Thompson to use their mosques to hold church parades.

In 1853, the British government signed the Perpetual Maritime Truce with the Arab rulers who oversaw the small, individual sheikdoms of Sharjah, Fujairah, Umm al-Qaiwain, Dubai, Abu Dhabi, Ras al-Khaimah, and Ajman. Because of that truce and the ensuing alliance between them and the British government, the seven sheikdoms became known as the "Trucial States" or the "Trucial Coast." Each sheikh who signed it agreed to its terms and to fly a red and white flag on his coastline to signal his alliance with the British. Hawley describes "three commandments" that the sheikhs had to now follow because of the treaty: The sheikhs would not commit piracy against British vessels; they would not commit piracy against one another; and they would not conduct business or diplomacy with any other powerful nation except for Great Britain. The last commandment was not enforced until later, in 1892.

The British alliance with the seven sheikhdoms made other countries uneasy. At the time, most of the Middle East was under the rule of the Ottoman Empire, which was worried about Great Britain's increasing role in what it considered to be its territory. By the 1870s, more Ottoman ships were sailing in the Arabian Gulf. At the same time, Persian rulers tried to establish their own connections and make their own agreements with the sheikhs of the Trucial States.

The British were so concerned that in 1887, they took steps to clarify their relationship with the sheikhs. A new agreement was signed, according to historian Mohammed Morsy Abdullah, which was "a written assurance that they [the sheikhs] would on no account correspond with or enter into an agreement with any government whatsoever, except the British, and that they would not, without the consent of the British [g]overnment, allow an agent of any other government to reside in their land." As other countries continued to try to intervene in the area, the British signed yet another agreement with the sheikhs in 1892. In that new treaty, explains Morsy Abdullah, "The [s]heikhs bound themselves, their heirs and their successors to abide by the assurances of 1887, and undertook on no account to cede, sell, mortgage or otherwise give for occupation any part of their territory save to the British [g]overnment."

Morsy Abdullah notes that the treaty of 1892 became the formal document that allowed Great Britain to officially become the authority in the Gulf region, which caused concern from other European nations. For example, France and Germany complained that the Gulf had become, in Abdullah's words, "a British lake." Also the Russians were alarmed by the British presence there and tried to undermine its political authority. Still, between 1904 and 1913, the French, German, Russian, and Ottoman governments all formally agreed not to challenge Great Britain's primacy in the Gulf.

FRICTION WITH THE BRITISH

The sheikhs of the seven emirates enjoyed many benefits from their alliance with the British government. One of these was the protection of their sheikhdoms and coastline by the British navy and military. In reaction, however, they felt that by the early 1900s, the British government had become too involved in their local affairs and tried to govern more closely than the sheikhs wanted. Great Britain installed an agent of its government in the Trucial States to oversee various issues and affairs that arose. In 1903, the British viceroy of India had addressed the sheikhs during a visit to the Gulf and said, "If any internal disputes occur, you will always find a friend in the British Resident, who

Although a treaty with the British Empire initially protected the sheikdoms of the local Arab rulers, the European superpower soon began to take advantage of the relationship. In order to control the flow of weapons in the area, the British began to deploy troops from an armed vessel to the sheik's coast *(above)*, an act that would escalate into something more serious.

will use his influence, as he has frequently done in the past, to prevent these dissensions from coming to a head, and to maintain the *status quo*, for we could not approve of one independent Chief attacking another Chief by land, simply because he has not been permitted to do it by sea, and thus evading the spirit of his treaty obligations."

In addition, many sheikhs felt stifled because the British set up a blockade in the Gulf to prevent the French, Germans, and Russians from trading arms. Many sheikhs benefited from those arms trades, and were angry about the incursion. They developed new methods of trading arms, such as using camels to carry arms overland as a way of avoiding the British blockade in the Gulf. In return, the British sent an armed naval ship to the coast in 1910 to monitor the coastline more closely. For many inhabitants and sheikhs, this was a sign that the British had a plan to colonize the sheikhdoms and tighten their control. As Morsy Abdullah notes, there was a cultural misunderstanding here as well. The British, he writes, "failed to understand that to the Arab his rifle is by far his dearest possession . . . because it is to him the only security for his life and property." No government then could preserve law and order in the Arabian Peninsula.

The British also did not consult the sheikhs before taking action in sending an armed vessel to their coastline. Part of the reason is the general sense of bias toward the sheikhs, who were viewed as culturally and morally inferior to the British. In 1908, British administrator and diplomat Percy Cox argued that a British agent should be placed in the Trucial States: "The experience of the last two or three years makes me doubt whether it is safe to leave these backward sheikhs longer in the charge of a native agent." Some of the sheikhs made the British nervous, including Sheikh Zayed bin Rashid, ruler of Abu Dhabi, who had violated the 1892 agreement by corresponding with the Persian government.

Cox and others tried repeatedly to install a British agent, but their attempts were refused by the ruler of Dubai, Sheikh Buti bin Suhail. There was already a resident agent—a person who reported to the British and acted in the interests of the British government—in the Trucial States, but he was a man of Arab descent. The British wanted an agent who was ethnically English there, perhaps because they felt they could trust him more. A local Arab would almost certainly have favored his own tribe, or its allies.

The refusals by the sheikhs to install a British agent were steady. Tension mounted on both sides until they exploded during what is called the "Dubai incident" of 1910. Dubai had become a major commercial and trading port by the early 1900s. In December of 1910, a British lieutenant, acting on information that some residents were hiding arms, conducted a search of their homes after seeking permission from Sheikh Buti bin Suhail. A few days later, a more extensive raid of homes was conducted by a British captain without seeking the sheikh's approval or permission. That raid on two homes of Dubai residents got out of control. Fights ensued, during which 12 Arabs were killed and more injured. As the British retreated to their ship, their comrades on board fired on the coastline to provide them with cover. The shelling killed another 25 Arabs.

The damage to the morale of the Arabs was tremendous, as was the damage done to the alliance between the sheikhdoms and the British government. Now, neither side trusted the other. The situation continued to escalate in the next few days, as the British insisted that Sheikh Buti bin Suhail allow a British agent to be installed in Dubai. Other demands by the British included the establishment of telegraph stations for British use, a post office, and the payment of a steep indemnity. The British threatened to bombard Dubai if these demands were not met, which would have ended the truce between the states and the British government. The sheikh refused some of the demands, including that of installing a British agent, but accepted others, and the incident passed without further violence.

The legacy of the Dubai incident, however, was that the sheikhs of the Trucial States no longer viewed Great Britain as an ally, but as an oppressor.

3

The Era of Petroleum and Independence

World War I revolutionized warfare in general, because of the advances in technology that were used in combat—from machine guns to tanks to bomber planes. It also signaled the fact that the world's most powerful nations—the United States, Great Britain, France and others—were growing more and more dependent on oil to fuel their machinery, including their land transport, tanks, naval vessels, and airplanes—and to keep their economies growing.

In 1859, oil had been struck successfully for the first time. Some oil wells had been built in Pennsylvania, Ohio, and Texas, but these would not suffice to meet the needs of the United States, which was in the midst of an industrial boom. Oil had been discovered in the Gulf region in 1908 after Persia (present-day Iran) had given a British oil company concessions to explore and drill on its land. Concessions were a formal contract; according to its terms, Persia received a set amount of money to allow the drilling, plus a percentage of the profits if oil were to be found. Soon, many other Middle Eastern nations and sheikhdoms were offering and selling concessions for drilling on their land. By the 1940s, it had become apparent that most of the oil reserves in the world were to be found right in the Middle East, in places like Kuwait, Saudi Arabia, Iraq, and others. Author P. Andrew Karam writes that a petroleum expert reported "the oil in this region is the greatest single prize in all history."

The sheikhs of the emirates were desperate to sell concessions for oil drilling since pearl diving had declined as a source of income by the 1920s. The Japanese had begun to develop cultured pearls, which could be produced and sold much more cheaply than by diving, which was a dangerous profession.

The oil boom in the United States occurred in several places, including Beaumont, Texas *(above)*. Oil was deemed so prosperous that when the big gusher was discovered the town's population increased from 9,000 to 30,000, seemingly overnight. While this would provide the basis for advancements in transportation, warfare, construction, and more, people soon realized the United States could not meet the demand for providing oil. The U.S. government and oil investors would soon turn to other countries and regions for their supply.

The British, who wanted to continue their authority over the Trucial Coast, believed that any concessions made by the sheikhdoms to drill on their land for oil should be made to the British government alone. They had begun to realize that the Trucial States were worth more to them than just a guardian of trade routes to India. Indeed, in 1919 India began rebelling against British rule, and the British people were growing tired of the cost of maintaining an empire. They doubted that oil, which had been found in Persia and Iraq, existed in sufficient quantities below the surface of the Trucial Coast, but they decided to act just in case. In 1922, the sheikhs agreed to give concessions for drilling to the British only, a move which angered the Americans. The Americans, however, gained concessions from other Middle Eastern countries, notably Bahrain and Saudi Arabia.

The British became alarmed when American oil companies began trying to negotiate with the sheikhs of the Trucial Coast in the 1930s. In fact, the Americans had struck oil in Bahrain in 1932. Morsy Abdullah writes, "The [s]heikhs were deeply impressed by the Americans' superior efficiency in the field of oil production, which for years to come influenced their willingness to co-operate with U.S. companies."

In the meantime, the British invested in the Trucial States in other ways. For example, civil aviation was a growing industry in the 1930s. Imperial Airways (the precursor to today's British Airways) was established in 1924 and was, according to its mandate, "the chosen instrument of the state for the development of air travel on a commercial basis." Five years later, one of its airplanes flew a successful flight from Great Britain to India—a stunning feat that confirmed the possibility of using aircrafts for commercial transportation to even the farthest corners of the British Empire.

The British wanted to have some control over land and air rights, not just at sea, but also in the Gulf, which was one of the main stops where British aircraft could stop to refuel. In 1932, the sheikh of Sharjah offered the British some of his land for aviation use, to land and launch aircrafts. Perhaps Sharjah's sheikh knew that the British were seeking out some land for this reason and had already made an offer to the sheikh of Ras al-Khaimah and been rejected. In any case, Sharjah's ruler ingratiated himself to the British with this offer, and in July of that year, a civil air agreement was signed between the British government and Sharjah. An airport and passenger house was built in Sharjah, the first British buildings to be erected on Trucial land. An air connection was soon made between London and Australia, and commercial and civil aviation received a tremendous boost. In 1937, Dubai also signed an aviation agreement, and another landing base was erected there for the use of British aircraft.

Other modernizations were implemented on the Trucial Coast, such as the establishment of the first post office—located in Dubai—in 1941. Before long, other post offices were built and, within several years, the individual states began issuing their own stamps. In the early 1950s, improved hospitals and modern schools were built. Roads connecting the states and cities were also laid down, and improvements were made to fresh water supply systems.

Still, the British wanted the Trucial States to sign oil agreements, so they found ways to make life difficult for the Emiratis. For example, the British stopped issuing travel papers to residents, making it difficult for residents to travel in and out of the Gulf. Eventually, the sheikhs complied. Dubai signed oil concessions with Great Britain in 1937, which lasted 75 years, and by 1938, the other sheikhs followed suit. Morsy Abdullah writes that the oil agreements "implied the extension of British protection on land as well as on sea." Nevertheless, the competition between the American (Standard Oil Company of California), British (British Petroleum and Petroleum Concession Ltd.), and French (Compagnie Francaise des Petroles) oil companies, continued over the next two decades.

In 1958, oil was discovered in Abu Dhabi, and everything changed.

PETRODOLLARS

The small land area known as the Trucial Coast became a priority on the lists of foreign powers squabbling for oil-drilling rights after deep reserves were found in Abu Dhabi. The attempt made in 1958 to find oil in Abu Dhabi was actually the second. The first attempt had failed as had other attempts made at Sharjah and other Trucial States. When oil was finally found in Abu Dhabi, it was described as a "nice sweet crude" by the petroleum engineer. By 1963, dozens of wells had been dug and 2.5 million tons of oil exported; in 1968, 23.6 million tons had been produced and exported—the pace of growth and production was dizzyingly fast.

Oil was then found in Dubai in 1966 and, in the following years, in the other small Trucial States. The sheikhs and the oil companies realized the importance of these discoveries. No longer would these be poor, desert kingdoms again. They had become nations sitting on a vast treasure.

The oil industry was a major boost to the economy—indeed, the influx of petrodollars was unprecedented. The profits were in the millions of British pounds, which were generally divided equally between the company and the sheikh. Morsy Abdullah explains that the oil companies dealt justly with the sheikhs:

> The oil industry "had become an international enterprise in which the oil-producing countries received a fair share. Negotiations and mutual respect of rights between both parties became the only guarantee for the British and foreign enterprises [to conduct business safely in the emirates] and not the presence of military forces, which offended national dignity and provided bitter attacks by Arab nationalists."

Arab nationalism had changed the political atmosphere of the Trucial States since World War II. Ten years before oil was discovered in Abu Dhabi, the state of Israel had been created by the United Nations after the British decided to end its rule in

Palestine. The creation of Israel in 1948 led to a refugee problem and the loss of land rights for 700,000 Palestinian Arabs, with whom the rest of the Arab world deeply sympathized. In Egypt, the rise of Gamal Abdel Nasser to the presidency also changed the political climate of the Middle East. A fierce opponent of Israel, Nasser called upon the Arabs to unite their countries and their strength. A sense of Arab nationalism, or pan-Arabism, in which people identified themselves as Arabs before their individual national identities, spread throughout the region. Intellectuals and common people vented pan-Arab sentiments, though they alarmed Arab leaders who sought to preserve their control over their national borders.

In the Gulf, the Trucial State Arabs also sympathized with the Palestinians and supported the fight for their rights. The Trucial States were swept by a powerful wave of Arab nationalism, which caused them to contribute money to Arab causes once petrodollars started to pour into their economies. Between 1948 and 1966, two wars and several skirmishes had broken out between Israelis and Arabs, and in 1967, Egypt, Syria, and Jordan declared war against Israel. In the Six-Day War, the Arabs had been defeated convincingly and more Palestinian territory had been captured by Israel. Morsy Abdullah writes that the 1967 defeat actually led to a further feeling of unity in the Arab world, and the Trucial States used their oil revenues to help pay for the losses sustained by the Arab states.

BRITISH ANNOUNCE DEPARTURE

In 1968, Great Britain announced it would end its authority on the Trucial Coast and allow the sheikhdoms to become independent. There were a number of reasons why the British left. By the early twentieth century, its empire had grown simply too large and had become too costly and difficult to administer. India declared its independence in 1947, and other colonies had been chipped away over the years. The British people were also growing more concerned about problems back home and

Zayed ibn Sultan al-Nahayan *(right)* descends from a long line of Abu Dhabi rulers, including his grandfather who shares his name. After the British left the area, Zayed emerged as a leader who could unite the other sheiks in the region to form a federation. Zayed became the first president of the United Arab Emirates.

the general sense was that the rest of the world should administer to their own affairs. Many British officials, however, regretted the decision to leave the Gulf, since it had done so much to modernize it, giving it a new future with the drilling and discovery of oil.

Once made, the decision was final. To their credit, the British worked to help the Trucial States administer themselves successfully after their planned departure in 1971, just three years after the decision was announced. As one British official said, "We owe it to the Gulf States as well as to ourselves to do the utmost in the time available." The Trucial sheikhs, to their credit, also sprung into action, especially Sheikh Zayed bin Sultan of Abu Dhabi.

On February 19, 1968, just one month after the British announcement that it would leave the Gulf in three years, the sheikhs of Abu Dhabi and Dubai proclaimed a union between their states. As Donald Hawley writes, "There would be a single flag and the [f]ederal [a]uthorities would deal with foreign affairs, and internal security, social and education services, nationality and immigration. The [f]ederal body would have legislative powers but matters not falling under its specific jurisdiction would remain the responsibility of the individual states." They saw that the British absence would create a vacuum in the relationships with the other sheikhdoms, as any problems that had arisen in the previous 150 years had been usually resolved by the British. A union with uniform clarified laws and policies would benefit their individual futures.

Abu Dhabi and Dubai invited many neighboring states, including Qatar, Bahrain, and the other sheikhdoms, to join their union. A few weeks later, a summit of these states was held in Dubai, and in theory, they all agreed to form the United Arab Emirates. Eventually, however, Qatar and Bahrain would declare their independence and abstain from joining the union. The emirates that remained were Dubai, Abu Dhabi, Umm al-Qawain, Ajman, Sharjah, Fujairah, and Ras al-Khaimah (which officially joined in 1972).

They created two levels of government: A supreme council consisted of all the rulers of the seven emirates who made laws, and a federation council gathered representatives of each emirate to enforce the laws handed down by the supreme council.

FATHER OF THE NATION

The supreme council's first head—and thus the first president of the United Arab Emirates—was Sheikh Zayed bin Sultan of Abu Dhabi. Born around 1920, he was the fourth son of Abu Dhabi's ruler, but perhaps the most politically savvy. He was named after his grandfather, the famous Sheik Zayed bin Sultan al-Nahyan, who ruled from 1855 to 1909. In keeping with Arab tradition, he spent his youth with Bedouins in the desert, learning their ways and traditions, which he respected. He also learned their ways of solving problems through consensus and dialogue, while always maintaining a feeling of brotherhood. Andrew Killgore writes that the Bedouin life taught young Zayed "the values of simplicity and lack of pretense, which he practiced all his life."

In 1946, he worked in government, taking an administration post and was very effective. His brother Sheikh Shahbut, was the sheikh of Abu Dhabi when oil was discovered, but Shahbut was reluctant to use petrodollars to develop the sheikhdom. He was deposed, and Zayed replaced him in 1966. Everyone was astounded and impressed by the level of improvement made to Abu Dhabi's infrastructure and domestic front during Sheikh Zayed's reign.

Most importantly, he shared the wealth of the petrodollars among the people of Abu Dhabi and the other sheikhs followed his example. Julia Wheeler wrote that Sheikh Zayed was "loved by the people of the Emirates, and respected by the expatriates who make up the vast majority of the population. This adoration goes beyond the sycophancy associated with many other Arab rulers. There is a real sense of gratitude for the sharing of wealth."

He is generally known as the architect of the union between Abu Dhabi and Dubai, and later of the union among the other emirates. During the months of meetings and talks leading up the formation of the UAE, he urged the sheikhs to think not only of their own territories but of the region in general. He asked them to imagine how much could be gained—and how much could be defended against outside aggressors—by pooling their resources together.

On December 2, 1971, the British officially abandoned the Trucial Coast. They left behind a jewel, glittering in the desert, which had just begun to transform itself into one of the most innovative, successful regions in the world.

4

Early Challenges to the New Nation

Early on, despite the pouring in of petrodollars to the economy of the fledgling UAE, its leaders knew that the oil their emirates sat on probably would not last forever. Almost from the beginning of their newfound wealth, the UAE's leaders began to diversify their economy, which meant looking for other ways to generate income. For example, their economic planners began exploring other sources of revenue, such as industry and tourism. These ideas would come into play much later in the UAE's young history.

It is not surprising that Sheikh Zayed, who was renowned for his belief in consensus and compromise, worked to promote a sense of unity among the Arab governments whose economies now depended on oil. Furthermore, in 1967 under Sheikh's Zayed's leadership, Abu Dhabi had become involved in the Organization of the Petroleum Exporting Countries (OPEC), whose mission is to "coordinate and unify the petroleum policies of [m]ember [c]ountries and ensure the stabilization of oil markets in order to secure an efficient, economic and regular supply of petroleum to consumers, a steady income to producers and a fair return on capital to those investing in the petroleum industry." OPEC was intended to formulate a common policy toward the oil companies and to protect the interests of the oil-producing nations when they negotiated with those companies.

In 1968, eight years after OPEC was established, Libya, Saudi Arabia, and Kuwait formed OAPEC, the Organization of Arab

Petroleum Exporting Countries, whose mission was distinct from OPEC's. "Established by an agreement amongst Arab countries which rely on the export of petroleum, the Organization of Arab Petroleum Exporting Countries (OAPEC) is a regional inter-governmental organization concerned with the development of the petroleum industry by fostering cooperation among its members. OAPEC contributes to the effective use of the resources of member countries through sponsoring joint ventures. The Organization is guided by the belief in the importance of building an integrated petroleum industry as a cornerstone for future economic integration amongst Arab countries."

Hoping to control the cost of oil to benefit the region instead of large oil corporations, OPEC was formed to create fairness in pricing, production, and supply in the oil industry. On December 25, 1973, members of OAPEC (the Arab members of OPEC) implemented an embargo on oil against nations that had supported Israel during the Yom Kippur War, resulting in the 1973 oil crisis.

The UAE wanted to be part of the political scene as well as the economic one, especially in the Arab world. It joined the United Nations (1971) and the Arab League (1972). The Arab League had been founded in 1945 by Egypt, Iraq, Lebanon, Saudi Arabia, Syria, Jordan, and Yemen, with headquarters in Cairo, Egypt. Its mission is to serve as a forum for the political, economic, cultural, and military concerns of its member states. The UAE's admittance into these organizations and involvement in diplomatic aid work signified its willingness to be an active player in Middle East and global politics.

Almost as soon as the UAE was established, politics triggered a situation that affected oil sales. In 1973, Israel and the Arab states entered yet another war over territory that Israel occupied during the 1967 war. OPEC had long determined to increase the share of oil profits its members received from the oil companies. At the same time, OAPEC, basically the Arab members of OPEC, decided to influence the outcome of the war by placing an embargo on those nations that supported Israel. The nations targeted for this were the United States and the Netherlands. Choosing the Netherlands was puzzling at the time, except that the port of Rotterdam does serve as a terminal for many oil shipments into the European countries, most of which were not sending arms to Israel during the war. Furthermore, oil production was cut at the same time that oil prices were raised (from $3 to over $5, and later, to over $11 per barrel), which nearly brought the economies of the Western nations, which depended on oil as their primary fuel source, to their knees.

The oil embargo was meant to punish the Americans and the Dutch for supporting Israel, and it worked, to some degree. In the United States, a country whose own oil reserves were almost exhausted but which depended on cheap gasoline to fuel its cars and industries, the economy suffered. Gas stations rationed the gas they sold to only 10 gallons per customer, companies shortened their work days, and all the states lowered their speed limits to 55 miles per hour. Within a few months, Western nations were experiencing severe unemployment, limiting automotive gasoline sales, and beginning to search for renewable sources of energy other than oil.

OAPEC ended its embargo in March 1974, but by then the importance of oil had been established. However, the Arab nations, including the UAE, agreed not to use oil again as a political weapon, especially since it failed to stop the United States from arming and supporting Israel and also because U.S. Secretary of State Kissinger was then mediating between Israel and both Egypt and Syria.

PROBLEMS WITH IRAN

The UAE's leaders knew that their seven tiny emirates had many vulnerabilities as a federation. According to the Library of Congress's country study of the emirates, "Because the UAE was a relatively small state, its leaders recognized that defending the country's security from both internal and external threats depended on skillful management of diplomatic relations with other countries, particularly larger and more powerful neighbors such as Iran, Iraq, and Saudi Arabia." In fact, challenges to its security arose almost immediately after its formation.

When the British announced they would leave the Gulf in 1968, another local power decided to act quickly to ensure its own dominance in the Gulf. Iran, formerly known as Persia, had benefited from the discovery of oil and petroleum exports in those early years. For centuries, Iran and the Arabs had quarreled over three small islands in the Gulf—Abu Musa, Greater Tunb, and Lesser Tunb. Muhammad Reza Shah also claimed that Bahrain, which was seeking independence in the 1970s, was legitimately a part of Iran, which caused the neighboring Arabs to fear a possible war once the British left.

The reasons for Iran's claims were clear: oil exports were rapidly enriching the Gulf region and the islands it claimed would allow it more control over the region, especially over the Strait of Hormuz, which connected the Persian Gulf to the Arabian Sea.

In 1970, Reza Shah Pahlavi, who had succeeded his father in 1941, recognized Bahrain's independence, giving up Iran's claim to the island. He also agreed to participate in a conference sponsored by Saudi Arabia on the issues of Gulf security and borders among its countries. However, on November 30, 1971, before the scheduled conference, Iran invaded and seized Abu Musa, owned by Sharjah, and Greater and Lesser Tunb, owned by Ras al-Khaimah. The military move surprised all the other Gulf States and angered Iran's neighbors. Moreover, those neighboring states realized that they needed to protect their territory and

Iraqi ruler Saddam Hussein (center, behind gun) invaded Iran in 1980, sparking an eight-year war between the two Arab countries. Instability in both countries, as well as border concerns and a problem with the Kurdish population, became hotly contested issues that resulted in war.

resources and so an arms race began in the Gulf. The conflict over the islands in the Strait of Hormuz would arise again in the early 1990s.

GULF WARS

Iran, however, remained a political problem in the Gulf. In 1979, Ayatollah Khomeini came to power in Iran, leading a revolution that caused Reza Shah Pahlavi to abdicate his throne and go into exile. One year later, Iran and Iraq started a devastating eight-year war for control in the Gulf. The two nations had been quarreling about their borders for many years, which Iraqi president Saddam Hussein used as a pretext for invading Iran from the south, in the province of Khuzestan.

Also, in 1981, the UAE joined the Gulf Cooperation Council (GCC), which was launched by Saudi Arabia. The other GCC members included Bahrain, Kuwait, Oman, and Qatar—all of which had also grown rich because of oil but wanted to resist outside intervention in their affairs. The UAE and other members realized that the Iran-Iraq War had brought much attention from the rest of the world to the Gulf. This was not surprising, given the dependence of the rest of the world on that region for its fuel resources. Saudi Arabia and the UAE worried that the Iran-Iraq conflict might cause other governments to over-step their boundaries. The GCC's primary aim was to establish standards and policies to prevent foreign meddling, or worse, invasion of their territories.

In August 1988, both Iran and Iraq finally accepted a United Nations resolution that called for each to pull back to its original border. During the eight years that the war raged, however, the UAE grew concerned about its various oil production sites, as well as its own relations with both Iran and Iraq. Dubai and Ras al-Khaimah, according to the Library of Congress country study of the UAE, "with a substantial number of Iranians and native Shia, leaned toward Iran." The study notes, however, that Abu Dhabi supported Iraq, which was not surprising given that emirate's commitment to Arab nationalism. In fact, Iran did attack Abu Dhabi for supporting its enemy. In 1987, a year before the war's end, Iranian missiles hit one of Abu Dhabi's oil facilities.

In 1990, Saddam Hussein threatened neighboring Arab country Kuwait by claiming that it was rightfully part of Iraq and thus should be reincorporated within Iraq's borders. This was an old dispute, one that originated during the British colonial era, when many borders of Arab countries were drawn. On August 2, 1990, Iraq did indeed invade Kuwait and took over its government. The military move—the first time an Arab state attacked and conquered another—shocked the Middle East region, its people, and governments. Arab leaders immediately called on Saddam Hussein to withdraw from Kuwait. When it became clear that Hussein would not withdraw, many Arab countries including the UAE and many UN member states, led by the United States, formed a coalition to force him to pull out of Kuwait. Operation Desert Storm was launched on January 17, 1991, with an aerial bombardment of Iraq that was, at that time, the longest and most intense example of aerial warfare in history. According to the Library of Congress, "United States aircraft bombed Iraqi positions from the UAE and United States ships, including aircraft carriers, operated out of UAE ports. The UAE air force also carried out strikes against Iraqi forces. A total of six UAE combat deaths were reported as a result of the fighting." Iraq surrendered quickly to the assault and withdrew from Kuwait in February 1991.

Once the war was over, the UAE insisted that it would not allow a foreign government to establish permanent military bases on its soil. This was one example of the UAE's consistent stand on remaining absolutely independent and free from control by other governments.

Iran and the UAE resumed their dispute in 1992 over who should control Abu Musa. Iran decided to expel all residents of Abu Musa who were not native-born Arabs, including foreign workers in many professions, such as teachers and doctors. They forced the expelled workers to first obtain an Iranian visa before letting them re-enter the island, angering the UAE government. The tiny island's major schools and medical clinics were run and operated by these foreign workers.

A couple of years later, Iran built an airport on Abu Musa and continues to occupy and control the island today. Iran's actions concern other countries because Abu Musa lies at the Strait of Hormuz, which is the main water artery leading into the Gulf. Potentially, Iran could blockade and close the opening to the Gulf in a time of high diplomatic tension. Furthermore, there have been reports that Abu Musa has large, untapped oil reserves.

In 1995, the UAE objected to the embargoes that the UN had placed on Iraq before and during the 1991 Gulf War. Sheikh Zayed permitted its embassy to reopen in Baghdad, and a few months later, Iraq reopened its embassy in the UAE. In speaking to the media, Sheikh Zayed stressed that the time had come for Arab states to make peace with Iraq and encouraged the UN to lift the global economic sanctions. The sanctions reportedly blocked humanitarian essentials, such as medicine, from reaching the country, leading to the deaths of millions of Iraqis. The sanctions had especially affected children, many of whom had died from malnutrition, diarrhea, disease, and other ailments.

In March of 2003, another attack was launched against Iraq. This time, the United States and, to a lesser extent, Great Britain, led the war with much less international support. There was also no mandate from the UN, as there had been for the 1991 war, to invade Iraq. According to the United States and British governments, the aim was to remove President Saddam Hussein from power because he had allegedly built up a powerful arsenal of what were termed "weapons of mass destruction." Later, this allegation was discovered to be false. Nevertheless, Iraq was defeated by May of that year, when U.S. president George W. Bush claimed that the mission had been accomplished. However, the resulting war in Iraq is far from over. While a new government has been established in Iraq, the country is in turmoil because of a raging civil war and sectarian violence. The number of casualties on both sides continues to climb. As of this writing, almost 4,000 U.S. soldiers have been killed in action, while over one million Iraqis (mostly civilians) are believed to have died from bombings, shootings, and other violence. Four million Iraqis have become refugees.

A TENSE ALLIANCE

The UAE opposed the 2003 invasion of Iraq from the beginning, as did some Western and most Arab governments. Still, as the Iraq War continues, the UAE maintains an alliance with the United States, allowing the U.S. Navy to use the busy port of Dubai for its military needs, as it lies strategically close to Iraq. It also provides the United States with oil, which is essential to the American economy.

In fact, after Israel, the UAE is probably the strongest and most important ally of the United States in the Middle East. For example, the UAE is one of the biggest importers of American products in the Middle East, importing almost $4 billion in food products alone, $100 million in medical equipment, $25 million in hardwood products, and $22 million in cosmetics and toiletries annually. Furthermore, it also imports manpower: the UAE is using much of its oil revenue to build world-class facilities and institutions in education, medicine, and technology. Thus, it advertises for American-educated engineers, doctors, teachers, and other professionals, promising high salaries and excellent work benefits. The rate of Americans moving to the Gulf in search of employment is rising; it is estimated that 20,000 Americans live and work in Dubai alone.

In other ways, though, the alliance is a tense and uncertain one. For example, when the Taliban, an ultra-conservative Islamic group, took over the government of Afghanistan and imposed a restrictive and terrorizing control over the country, the UAE was only one of three countries to formally and diplomatically recognize it. (The other two were Saudi Arabia and

Pakistan). While this fact usually causes some people to criticize the UAE , others note that the UAE actually provided the United States with important intelligence about the Taliban, with which the United States had no direct communication.

Other tensions have arisen recently. In early 2006, it was announced that Dubai Ports World (DPW), a major company in the Gulf that is owned by the emir of Dubai, was buying the rights to manage six American ports in large cities. The result was a shameful outbreak of anti-Arab sentiment and racism in

When news was made public that a Dubai company, Dubai Ports World, was buying up ports in the United States, protests were held in opposition of the sale *(above)*. The anti-Arab feelings resulting from the September 11 tragedies in 2001 were on display, causing tension between the United States and the United Arab Emirates.

the United States, exploited by many politicians. Control of the American seaports already rested with a foreign company, Peninsular and Oriental Steam Navigation Company (P&O), managed in Great Britain, which was bought by DPW in March 2006. Part of the sale included the management contracts of those American ports, which included New York, New Jersey, Philadelphia, New Orleans, Baltimore, and Miami, as well as 16 other ports. The American government, under President George W. Bush, approved the sale; however, allegations that the United States was selling its national security to an Arab country quickly filled news headlines, and the controversy even became an issue for Congressional debate. Democratic New York Congressman Chuck Shumer held a press conference about the issue, which helped spread the information and made it a national news item.

The debate raged for several weeks, with the loyalty of the UAE to U.S. interests publicly called into question. Susan Collins, the Republican senator from Maine and the chairwoman of the Senate Government Affairs and Homeland Security Committee, said that though "the UAE is an ally in the war on terrorism, the country has historically been used as a base of terrorist operations and financing." Many critics of the sale pointed out that two of the hijackers who attacked the United States on September 11, 2001, were from the UAE. Still others pointed out that those two men had been trained in others countries, despite being UAE nationals.

President Bush argued that to block the deal would be an insult to the UAE, a major ally of the United States. He also threatened to veto any action by Congress to block the deal. Still, the Appropriations Committee in the House of Representatives did block the sale. The chairman of the committee, Jerry Lewis, said, "The amendment is straight-forward and is a rifle shot crack to block the Dubai Ports World deal only. This is a national issue. This is a national security bill. We want to make sure that the security of our ports is in America's hands." Soon after, the Democrats also introduced a bill in the Senate to block the sale.

Many claimed that the attack on the sale of the port's management was really a criticism of the Bush administration, but the issue was not likely to just fade away. Eventually, DPW sold the management rights to those ports in question to an American company, American International Group, so the issue seemed settled. Unfortunately, the controversy raised tensions between the two nations. It also drew attention to the existence of anti-Arab feeling within the United States, since it was unlikely that the sale would have caused a stir if any other foreign company had purchased it.

5

Religion and Traditions of the UAE

Accoring to the country's constitution, Islam is the official religion of the United Arab Emirates. All aspects of life are affected by Islamic traditions and practices. Nonetheless, the country's laws encourage toleration of all religions. Because of the presence of guest workers, most residents of the country are, in fact, citizens of other countries; consequently, a variety of other religions are represented in the country as well. According to the U.S. Department of State's 2007 International Religious Freedom Report, the citizens of the country are mostly Sunni Muslim, and only 15 percent are Shi'a Muslims. About four percent of the population practices either Christianity or Buddhism. Hindus, Parsis, Baha'is, and Sikhs also call the emirates home, especially because half the UAE population consists of South Asian immigrants working and living there, at least temporarily. Eighty percent of the people living in the UAE are foreign.

Because Islam is the state religion, the government provides financial assistance to most mosques. Sunni leaders, or imams, are employees of the state, supervised and compensated by the government. Only a few Sunni mosques in the UAE are private. On the other hand, all Shi'a mosques are private and are maintained by the Shi'as themselves, rather than by the government, though government funds are granted on occasion and upon request. This may be a result of geographical circumstances;

whereas Sunni Muslims live throughout the country, most of the Shi'a Muslims live in the northern emirates.

The government body that oversees the practice of Islam in the emirates is the General Authority for Islamic Affairs and Endowments. This organization has many tasks. The authority

Unlike other countries where the majority of the population belongs to one religion, the United Arab Emirates encourages diversity within their borders, particularly in religion. Their widespread acceptance of other faiths and celebrations, including Christmas *(above)*, has made them a regional and international model for tolerance.

aims to promote Islamic culture, closely supervises the practice of the state religion, and regularly issues information to imams and provides the mosques with whatever they need to serve the people. This organization also takes responsibility for coordinating the training and licensing of imams and prayer callers, licensing of worship sites and pilgrimage campaigns, planning and running religious summits and meetings, reviewing printed materials, and managing and promoting financial investment in the faith. Members of the clergy are expected to adhere to the guidance of the supervising organization; sermons are carefully monitored. Furthermore, as the official religion, Islam is taught in the public and private schools for Muslim children. No other religion may be taught in the public schools.

The United Arab Emirates is considered by many people to be a model for other countries that wish to promote a tolerant atmosphere among citizens of diverse faiths. People of non-Muslim faiths may, in general, practice their religions without persecution from the government or other citizens. Although it is illegal for missionaries to try to convert people to faiths other than Islam, the government does permit missionaries to perform humanitarian work in the country. Furthermore, non-Muslim denominations may build and operate churches with the permission of the local ruler. To do so, they must apply for and receive a land grant from the ruler of the emirate in which they wish to practice their faith. People of other religious denominations may run their communities as they see fit as long as they act in accordance with the law. They may also operate their own parochial schools where they may include religious instruction.

As the national religion, the Islamic tradition of the UAE contributes to the laws that govern citizens' daily activities. Criminal and domestic disputes, for example, are settled in the Islamic, or Shari'a, courts. Shi'a Muslims, however, may take family disputes to a Shi'a council instead of the Islamic court. While citizens who are charged with crimes do come before a

Shari'a court, the judge may provide civil rather than religious punishments. Furthermore, non-Muslims may appeal consequences from Shari'a courts, and they may be overturned.

Muslims and non-Muslims who are incarcerated may benefit in a variety of ways from learning about Islam. Prisoners who become Muslims may have their sentences reduced. Memorizing the Koran can help prisoners to earn money, reduce their sentences, and possibly receive pardons, depending on the rules of the emirate in which they live. (These options are not offered to people serving life sentences.) Moreover, people convicted of lesser offenses are occasionally pardoned on religious holidays.

Certain religious holidays are also considered national holidays. The month of Ramadan for example, is observed throughout the country. During Ramadan, Muslims fast and pray from dawn to sunset and smoking, drinking, and eating in public during the day are forbidden. Other denominations' rights are respected in similar fashion. Businesses are permitted to serve non-Muslims and decorate and advertise for non-Muslim holidays provided they do not interfere with observance of Ramadan. The Islamic tradition of tolerance is encouraged.

The United Arab Emirates has drawn praise from religious leaders and visitors from around the world. Among those who have commended the emirates are the Romanian ambassador, representatives from the Coptic Church, the former Roman Catholic Archbishop of Washington, the Archbishop of Canterbury, the Latin Patriarch of Jerusalem, and groups from the American Anti-Defamation League and the American Jewish Committee. Furthermore, the rulers of the individual emirates generously donate land to those who wish to create new houses of worship, non-Muslim as well as Muslim. In addition, they hold a number of symposiums to further strengthen ties among those who practice different faiths. Clearly, the rulers continue to demonstrate their interest in a tolerant society through a variety of actions.

SOCIAL CUSTOMS

Since the emirates developed from different tribes, and each tribe had varying customs and practices, it is not surprising that the seven emirates also have different views on social customs. On one extreme, Sharjah has very strict codes about social propriety. In 2001, the Supreme Council of the emirate passed the Decency and Public Conduct Rules and Objectives, or what is commonly known as the Sharjah Decency Laws, which forbid single men and women from socializing publicly together. Furthermore, men and women must dress conservatively in public. For example, men cannot wear short shorts or go out bare-chested in public, while women must wear clothing that covers their backs, stomachs, and hair. While these values of dress and behavior are traditional throughout the Muslim world, they are more strictly enforced in Sharjah. The laws were passed in an attempt to protect both residents and tourists against what the police chief of Sharjah referred to as "imported values."

In Fujairah, social norms are dictated completely by the emir, who governs differently from his neighbors. The ruler of Fujairah owns all the land in the emirate personally, so his word is final in all matters. He governs strictly and adheres to a conservative view of Muslim law. While drinking is not allowed, in accordance with Shari'a, some hotels catering to foreign tourists may serve liquor to their guests. However, public decency is enforced. According to one informational Web site, "On many Fridays, one can still witness lashes meted out for minor offences, such as being drunk in public, with the unfortunate victims usually from the poorer segments of society. Punishments such as these are delivered outside the main court, located next to Fujairah Tower, in the centre of the city."

Throughout their history, society in the UAE has been extremely family-oriented. As such, marriage holds great importance to citizens of the emirates. Before oil was discovered, marriages were arranged within tribes. Now, although people are free to choose their mates, many citizens still want marriages arranged by parents or other tribal members. In recent years, in order to strengthen the native culture and limit foreign influences, there has been a government effort to persuade male citizens to marry UAE women rather than seek brides from out of the country or from among those expatriates who live in the emirates. This may be a challenge because so many of the people who live in the UAE are foreign nationals. To encourage citizens to marry each other rather than foreigners, thereby strengthening Emirati society, the president of the UAE instituted the marriage fund in 1994 to ease financial hardship for couples who wish to marry. Young men who marry women from the emirates receive a substantial grant from the marriage fund. Although Islam permits men to have four wives, most men marry only one.

The family unit is changing as well. Traditionally two or more generations shared a domicile as an extended family. Now, however, only parents and children normally live together in one house, and domestic servants help with domestic chores and childrearing. Although they no longer live in the same home, citizens generally live near their parents and other relatives. In addition to living near their family members, people tend to choose homes appropriate for their social standing and background. Citizens generally do not live near immigrants. An average Emirati family has two servants, and despite concerns regarding foreign influences on children, most servants come from abroad. The government encourages people to have large families, and the average family has six to eight children, though that number is declining.

Just as home and family customs are changing, the way people work is also in transition. Before people in the emirates made significant amounts of money on oil, people earned their living through fishing, farming, pearl diving, and related businesses, and some may have been nomads, herding camels, sheep, and goats. Today, however, the oil business has brought many jobs to the emirates. In addition, the government has been investing in businesses other than oil and natural gas. Citizens are generally employed by the government in a variety of service departments. Many work in schools or government offices, or they serve as police officers or soldiers. Women who work often use childcare facilities at their workplaces if they do not have domestic servants to watch their children.

The economic development in the United Arab Emirates has led to the prosperity of many citizens, but also has created more jobs for people in the country. In order to satisfy the demand for labor, the country has welcomed foreigners to supply the workforce for the oil and construction industries *(above)*. Because of this, foreign workers make up a larger part of the population than the citizens of the UAE.

Traditionally Emiratis worked from around eight in the morning until lunchtime. Then they would have a long break and return to work in the late afternoon or evening. The largest meal of the day was traditionally the mid-day meal, so people would often return home to dine with their families and then take naps. While some jobs still accommodate this traditional schedule, others have moved to a schedule more similar to that used in the United States, from eight in the morning until five in the evening. The work week varies according to industry as well. Some retail stores are open every day, but many businesses and shops are open from Sunday through Thursday and closed on Friday and Saturday. Because Friday is the Muslim day for communal worship, most people are off for all or part of the day.

TRADITIONAL FOODS

Traditional foods in the UAE are similar to those in other Arab countries, with a few notable extras. Because of its geographical location on the water, several varieties of grilled fish, including grouper, mackerel, and mullet, have traditionally been eaten in the region, Muslims are not permitted to eat pork but lamb is common. Restaurants do not even serve pork although they do make an effort to provide substitutes for non-Muslims.

International foods and restaurants are plentiful, from Italian, to French, to Chinese, to Indian. In that sense, the UAE is a haven for international cuisine lovers because some of the finest chefs in the world cater to clientele in first-class restaurants in the emirates. Another reason for such diversity in cuisine is the fact that only 15 to 20 percent of the residents of the UAE are native citizens—the rest are foreign-born workers or expatriates from various nations around the world.

Nevertheless, some foods and customs are unmistakably Arab. Two of the most popular sandwiches are the *shawarma* sandwich, similar to a Greek gyro, in that finely sliced and well-spiced lamb is rolled into a sheet of Arabic or pita bread, then topped with a white sauce and other condiments, and the falafel sandwich, which is made by frying patties of chick peas and spices to be served on Arabic bread with vegetables and sauces.

Arab cuisine also includes *hummus*, a creamy dip made with sesame oil, garlic, and lemon juice that is eaten by scooping it with slices of Arabic bread. Another popular dip is *foul mudammas*, a dip like hummus, but made with fava beans, as well as *baba ganoush*, a dip made with creamed eggplant. Hummus, foul mudammas, and baba ganoush are usually served as part of *mezze*, a selection of dishes that starts off a meal, like an appetizer. Other dishes commonly offered on a mezze platter are *tabbouleh*, or a finely chopped salad of tomatoes, onions, parsley, and couscous, and *warak einab*, a "finger food" made with meat and rice rolled into grapevine leaves.

In terms of main entrees, nothing in Arab cuisine compares in terms of social import to the *mansaff* platter. Served at major events, including weddings and funerals, the meal consists of a whole roasted lamb served on a bed of rice. The significance of the meal comes from the fact that lamb is expensive and thus reserved for special occasions. Another popular local treat is *ads*, or lentils, served as a soup or cooked with rice. *Makbous* is a type of lamb casserole that is widely enjoyed.

Arabic coffee is an important culinary as well as cultural item. Coffee grounds are roasted so that the coffee produced is rich and dark; water is boiled three times and the grounds are stirred in slowly. If the event is a happy one, such as a wedding or an engagement or a child's birth, sugar is also stirred in, and the coffee is served either *mazbut* (medium) or *ziyada* (with extra sugar). If the event is sad, then the coffee is served *saadah*, or plain and unsweetened. The coffee is also typically flavored with cardamom, a spice native to the East. It is made in a small metal or enamelware pot with a long handle and served in small demitasse (literally, "half cup") cups that do not have handles. A common tradition is for drinkers to turn their empty cups upside down in their plates so that the grounds slide down the sides. After the grounds dry, people try to read their fortunes in the pattern created in the sides of the cup. The way that coffee is served is also culturally prescribed. A host or hostess will serve the coffee on a tray and hand the cups to the eldest person in the room first, then continue serving to guests according to their age until the youngest and last person has his or her cup.

As a side note, a popular item of Arab consumption is the *shisha*, or hookah pipe. Not all restaurants offer this smoking pipe, so usually people can smoke it specifically in a shisha cafe. In recent years, this ancient smoking pipe, with flavored tobacco inhaled through boiling water at the base, has enjoyed a resurgence in popularity.

6

Women in the UAE

In 1975, women's organizations throughout the emirates united to create the UAE Women's Federation under the leadership of Sheikha Fatima bint Mubarak, wife of the country's leader, Sheikh Zayed. As chairperson of the federation, Sheikha Fatima helped advance the rights of her fellow countrywomen.

Initially, the organization sought to help women learn to read and write and learn about the world so that they could improve life for their families. This was a major step since before the oil boom illiteracy rates in the emirates were high among both men and women, but it was not seen as imperative for women to be educated. Now, the Women's Federation seeks to help women in the UAE improve not only their own situations but also to contribute to life in the emirates. Another major step was taken in 1983 when Sheikh Zayed said that women should not be limited to childrearing.

The Women's Federation operates committees that focus on education, religion, parenting, social life, culture, sports, history, and the arts. There are currently 31 branches scattered throughout the emirates. The branches provide opportunities for women to become literate; learn about their country's history and religion; develop childrearing skills; receive occupational training; learn to manage a household; and participate in a variety of social, athletic, and cultural activities. In addition, women are encouraged to avail themselves of the educational opportunities to which they are entitled as citizens of the UAE. In addition to a number of public and private institutions where women may obtain training and earn degrees, the government formed an institution to meet the unique needs

Cheri Booth, wife of former British prime minister Tony Blair, delivers a speech during the 2006 Women as Global Leaders Conference at Zayed University. Founded to provide higher education to the women of the United Arab Emirates, Zayed University has two campuses and a broad undergraduate program. With 3,200 students, the university is one of the UAE's biggest steps in equalizing opportunities between men and women in the emirates.

of female students in a society where women traditionally had not attained high levels of formal education. In 1998, Zayed University was created solely to educate Emirati women, and it continues to expand.

In addition to education, in recent years the Women's Federation has focused on marriage and its importance to society. In the past 20 years, many women have remained unmarried for a variety of reasons. At first, that may have been a result of diverse educational backgrounds. It is possible that men wanted to marry women who had educational backgrounds equal to theirs, but in previous years, few women were educated to the same degree as men. If this is the case, the future may hold the reverse problem. At present in the UAE, many females' educational achievements equal or surpass those of the males.

Another reason for the increasing number of unmarried women in the emirates is the high cost of a wedding. As incomes have risen, the cost of an elaborate celebration has risen as well. In Arab culture, weddings hold a very important place and are usually celebrated with much pomp and ceremony. Furthermore, the demand for a large dowry has increased. As a result, many men have chosen to marry foreign brides, leaving women from the UAE unmarried. One cause, until recently, is that UAE men were far more likely than women to go abroad for advanced professional or technical training just when they reached marriage age and hence married foreign women. In an attempt to remedy this situation, the government instituted the Marriage Fund. Men who intend to marry but are financially unable to do so are eligible for these funds provided they choose to marry young women from the UAE. Because of the stability marriage brings to society, the Women's Federation encourages people to avail themselves of the government-provided services, including the Marriage Fund, the creation of halls dedicated to hosting wedding celebrations at a cost lower than the fees charged at a luxury hotel, and the government's support for the practice of demanding lower dowries.

Another issue is that older men will marry younger women from outside the country. The Women's Federation discourages this practice because these younger women come to the United Arab Emirates with little education, and they are not able to contribute much to the society of their new country. In the past few years, the government has worked with women's groups in a concerted effort to curtail the practice of marrying foreign wives. For example, Marriage Fund grants are not available to men who take foreign wives. Older men are discouraged from taking wives from abroad because those women often want to marry for financial reasons. Furthermore, people studying on government scholarships are also prohibited from marrying while in the emirates.

Government officials and leaders of the Women's Federation hope to decrease the number of marriages between UAE nationals and foreign-born wives because of what it sees as the negative effects these marriages have on UAE society. Marriages between UAE nationals and foreign-born wives are more likely to end in divorce, which can be difficult for children. Furthermore, in the past men who married foreigners would marry women from India or from other Arab countries. The practice has now expanded to include women from all over the world. This may be a result of religious tradition; Islamic women traditionally have had little contact with men in daily life and therefore had little or no contact with potential mates. Now, however, men in the UAE may deal with many expatriate women on a daily basis and form relationships. It is also possible that the increase in the number of women attaining higher education is adversely affecting the number of marriages between UAE citizens. Women who are heavily committed to pursuing their educations and furthering their careers may find little time to concern themselves with marriage and family matters. The government and the Women's Federation discourage the marriages between nationals and expatriates and believe that marriages between citizens will strengthen the UAE society.

According to some accounts, the UAE has the highest divorce rate in the Gulf. In 2005, it reached 46 percent. Many marriages between citizens and foreign women end in divorce, often leaving the women with the tasks of raising the children and earning a living. While women who are nationals receive assistance after divorce, foreign women are not eligible for all of the same government programs as the nationals, which can make life very difficult for these women. In addition, the women are not free to leave the country unless they leave their children in the UAE. Consequently, many choose to stay despite the financial hardship they encounter.

The federation also discourages the practice of hiring domestic servants from other countries. As women have entered the job market, they have found a need for help in caring for their children and homes. The Women's Federation sees this practice as harmful to society and potentially harmful to the family. The organization is currently working to publicize this problem in hopes of convincing women to raise their own children or find domestic childcare. In addition, the organization hopes to increase the number of childcare options, which might alleviate the need to have foreign nannies caring for UAE citizens' children. UAE women who have tried to put their children in childcare have faced many of the same issues as Western women. Children get sick, work schedules change, and family members may be critical or uncooperative. Therefore, the government is working to make childcare more accessible to working mothers. For example, the Women's Federation and other women's organizations have promoted legislation to provide childcare in the work place in order to help women combine their roles as productive citizens and mothers.

In addition to the committee's work to increase the number of marriages in society, the organization has actively contributed to the pursuit of women's rights not only in the emirates themselves, but also throughout the world by participating in major international women's conferences. The federation believes that Islam provides women in the UAE certain rights, and their experience could serve as a model for women in other countries. Women in the UAE enjoy the same rights to titles, education, and professions that men enjoy. The constitution guarantees these rights as well as pay equal to men, and women participate in all aspects of society, from commerce to the military to government to education.

One current goal of the federation is to encourage more women in the UAE to seek employment. In the past, educated or not, women tended to give up their jobs once they had children. Furthermore, because most citizens were Muslims, most women avoided fields that would require face-to-face communication

The Women's Federation of the United Arab Emirates encourages women to continue working outside the home after having children. The organization has lobbied the government to provide childcare for working mothers, as well as foreign-born women who have children in the UAE. The federation's efforts and increased access to education has allowed more women in the UAE to take on nontraditional employment in science, technology, and even with the police force *(above)*.

with men. Now, more women are pursuing careers and remaining in the work force even after having children. Women are well represented in fields which have traditionally attracted them, including education, health care, and social services. The number of women in scientific and technological fields is growing, as is the number of women in business. This is partly due to the fact that education is readily available to all citizens. The media also deserves some credit for the increase in the number of women in the work force. Many women work in the media, and colleges and universities market communications courses to continue to encourage women to work in the field. There are women in the police departments in the UAE in a variety of jobs. In addition, women are working in the military in all capacities except those which would put them in the front lines.

Currently, women comprise approximately 22 percent of the work force. Sixty-six percent of government employees are women, and 30 percent of those government jobs are super-visory positions. These numbers demonstrate an immense improvement since the formation of the UAE, when very few women worked outside the home. Even in 1985, the federal government reported that the work force was only 10 percent female. Despite these strides, there is still room for improve-ment. Many women remain unemployed because they or their families do not think it is appropriate for them to interact with men to whom they are not married or related. Others choose not to take jobs because their husbands fear they will neglect their domestic duties. Men also feel their status as providers is threatened if their wives hold paying jobs. Finally, other women are well-educated, but they are trained in the "wrong" fields, those for which there is little demand. According to Sheikha Lubna al-Qasimi, UAE Economy Minister, business is growing in the UAE, and liberal arts degrees are not necessarily sought by companies. In addition to business, those skilled in information science are needed as well. Re-training is provided by the government to decrease the unemployment rate.

RELIGION AND THE ROLE OF WOMEN

Many people in the West have a negative stereotype of Islam and the practices of an Islamic society. Some people even equate Islam with the suppression of women. Western media often depict Muslim women covered in black cloaks, or hijabs, and face veils as if to portray the way that Islam allegedly oppresses women.

The UAE is a deeply religious and conservative society. Yet, many women in the UAE do not believe that the Islamic religion obstructs their path to happiness. In fact, many see sources of women's empowerment in the Koran. For example, Islam was the first of the three monotheistic religions (the others being Judaism and Christianity) that granted women the right to inherit, own, and sell property. Islam granted women the right to own and manage businesses, as in the case of the Prophet Muhammad's first wife, Khadija, thus giving them the right to work and earn an income. It is often pointed out by many critics of this negative view of Islam that, at the time that Islam was spreading throughout the Middle East, Asia, and Africa, women in Europe and other Western nations were still not given a voice in politics and society.

In terms of education, scholars of Islam point out that the Prophet Muhammad was credited with saying, "The pursuit of knowledge is a duty of every Muslim, man and woman." Furthermore, a Muslim woman was given the right to choose her spouse, or at least reject the spouse chosen for her by her parents, although in practice this was rare, and, if the marriage did not work out for specific reasons, she could initiate divorce proceedings against her husband (although this, too, was rare). This was quite revolutionary for this time period, and it explains why many Muslim women find their religion to be a liberating force. While many Muslim countries and governments have perhaps neglected to enforce some of these religious laws, they nevertheless exist in the Islamic tradition.

Perhaps the most controversial of Islamic traditions is the permission for men to practice polygamy. How can women be viewed as equal to men, critics charge, when a man can marry up to four wives? Indeed, in some parts of the Persian Gulf and specifically in the UAE, the practice of polygamy continues to exist. Yet again, a closer reading of the actual law permitting polygamy is important. The Koran states, "Marry the women of your choice, one, two, three, or four. But if you fear that you shall not be able to deal justly with them, then marry only one." Many interpret the Prophet Muhammad's words to mean that polygamy—which was widely practiced and unregulated before the dawn of Islam—was actually discouraged by the Prophet. He actually said that it would be impossible for a man to treat all his wives equally, though he did try. In fact, historically, when Islamic forces were engaged in battle and many of the Prophet's soldiers were dying, widows were left sometimes unable to provide for themselves and their children. Some suggest that the marriage of up to four women was meant to help alleviate this social problem. In any case, polygamy in the UAE is very rare today, as most men marry only one woman. Indeed, in some cases, women write into their marriage contract that their husbands-to-be are not permitted to take other wives as long as they are still alive and still married to them.

Women in the UAE, however, view their roles in society differently than many Western women. Emirati women value their independence, but many believe that the family should play a significant role in their lives. For that reason, Emirati women usually agree with their society about the value of being good wives and mothers, as well as finding a good balance between family life and their careers. Furthermore, over 99 percent of Emirati girls receive an education because the popular belief is that, even though a woman may choose not to have a career, her education will nevertheless benefit her children. In that sense, becoming educated is more of a civil obligation or a duty to the nation and the family than to oneself.

7

Education and Economy

Before the UAE was formed, very few people in the region had access to formal education. Consequently, after the oil business brought prosperity to the emirates, Sheikh Zayed was determined that the Emirati would be educated so that they would be able to use their resources wisely. The UAE guarantees education for male and female citizens and requires that all children attend school through the secondary level. Today, many more students opt to attend colleges or universities either at home or abroad.

Students begin education with kindergarten at age 4 or 5, and they continue into primary school, which they attend from ages 6 to 12. State schools and many private schools are single-sex, though some schools catering to Western families are co-educational. The preparatory school educates students from ages 12 to 14 or 15, and the secondary school completes the education for students ages 15 to 17 or 18. Upon completing their requirements, students take an exam in order to receive the Shahadat Al-Thanawiya Al-Amma. Some students opt to attend a technical secondary school from age 12 through 18. The government aims to "emiratize" the primary and secondary schools by 2020; the suggestion is that native teachers are more likely to protect Islamic beliefs and regional customs taught to students.

In kindergarten and the primary grades, students enjoy a 1 to 20 student to teacher ratio. In the preparatory and secondary grades, the ratio is 1 to 15. Expatriate students may attend public schools for a fee, or they may attend one of the many private schools catering to expatriates including Egyptian, Indian, Palestinian, British, and American. Despite the number of public schools available, nearly 40 percent of the Emirati send their children to private schools. Some of these private schools are foreign language schools that enroll expatriate children as well as nationals. Generally, students attend schools four to six days each week. Students attend school in the fall and spring with a short mid-winter break and a longer summer break. The schedule is modeled on the British schedule, but modifications have been made to suit the extremely hot, dry climate. Consequently, the summer break is longer, and school days have been extended throughout the rest of the year to make certain that students have sufficient time for learning.

One goal of the educational system is to ensure that students graduate with technological skills. To that end, there is a computer for every 10 students in kindergarten, one for every five in primary schools, one for every two in preparatory schools, and one computer for every student in the university. In addition, the Ministry of Education continues to develop computer training programs to ensure that UAE nationals can compete with their counterparts in other parts of the world.

Not only are students guaranteed education through the primary and secondary levels, but they may find more opportunities in local colleges and universities. In addition to its extensive public school system, the UAE has a well-developed system of higher education. Ninety-five percent of women and 80 percent of men seek education after the secondary level. Students who wish to attend school in the United Arab Emirates may attend United Arab Emirates University (UEAU) which opened in 1977. UEAU offers an impressive array of undergraduate degrees and graduate programs, and many are accredited by international bodies. In addition, UEAU offers a variety of professional programs that are evaluated periodically to ensure that they are competitive with other programs in the world.

Because many of its citizens were uneducated before the oil boom, the United Arab Emirates is determined to provide an exceptional educational program for its society. The government emphasizes technological skills and students begin using computers in kindergarten, while adults benefit from training workshops.

In addition to UEAU, students may choose to attend one of the Higher Colleges of Technology (HCT). The HCT is the largest provider of higher education in the emirates; men's and women's campuses throughout the UAE supply technological education to students in the UAE on modern sites featuring the latest equipment and techniques of instruction. Leaders in UAE business firms consult as programs are developed to align academic standards with the needs of the workplace. Many programs are offered in English, and students are required to participate in work in their chosen field in order to earn their degrees. With cooperation from partners, many students obtain internships, cultural knowledge, and language development opportunities from companies abroad and in the UAE. The HCT's high standards have given them a reputation for producing skilled graduates who can communicate with others, demonstrate technological competence, and adapt to unforeseen situations. Consequently, these graduates are actively sought by employers, especially those hoping to emiratize their work force.

Zayed University is another public institution of higher education. ZU was established in 1998 as a women's college for UAE nationals and has campuses in Abu Dhabi and Dubai. Most instruction is offered in English, but graduates must also be fluent in Arabic. Five colleges comprise the university, including Arts and Sciences, Business Sciences, Communication and Media Sciences, Education, and Information Technology. In addition to fluency in English and Arabic, goals for students include technological competence, research skills, professional behavior, and leadership ability. The university hopes to produce graduates who will affect all areas of life in the emirates in the future, so undergraduate education is one focus of the institution's efforts. The school plans to add graduate programs to its offerings in the future. Furthermore, in the coming years Zayed University will focus on research in order to maximize its role in the growth of the UAE.

Students who do not wish to attend the public universities may select from several private colleges and universities. The Center for Excellence in Applied Research and Technology is a private division of the HCT, and it currently provides private education to the greatest number of students in the Middle East. This branch of the HCT cooperates with many corporate partners, such as IBM, to develop technological advancements in a variety of fields, including genetics and biotechnology. In CERT

Technology Park are offices of Intel, Honeywell, and Lucent Technologies. CERT provides undergraduate and graduate education and invests in research in the private sector to maintain an awareness of and an ability to respond to the needs of employers.

Other private universities in the UAE include the American Universities of Sharjah and Dubai. Students might also choose to attend Ajman University of Science and Technology, Abu Dhabi University, or Al Hosn University. There is even a branch of the Sorbonne, France's famed University of Paris, in Dubai.

The UAE continues to expand the educational opportunities offered to its citizens. Dubai has created a new center for such educational opportunities. The campus of Dubai Knowledge Village will be approximately one kilometer long and host branches of universities from many countries, including the United States, England, Ireland, Belgium, Australia, India, Pakistan, and Iran. In addition, the center hosts human resource centers, professional development and other types of training centers. In addition to a wide variety of foreign universities, Dubai Knowledge Village is host to distance learning companies, e-learning providers, and corporate learning companies. To make the site attractive to partners, the UAE has guaranteed many benefits. Foreign business firms will own their companies completely and keep all of their profits. Partners will not pay taxes nor experience difficulty in obtaining visas.

Dubai Knowledge Village is not the only place where students may obtain an education from a foreign institution. Many American universities are opening branches in the UAE for a variety of reasons. First, the American system of higher education has long been considered the best in the world in many areas. For years, students have traveled to nearby American universities in Beirut, Lebanon, or Cairo, Egypt, or they have traveled to the United States itself to obtain degrees in American universities—some remaining in America afterward, but many returning home with their degrees, knowledge, and professional contacts in hand. Many seek the high-tech knowledge for which

American universities are so well known. Some want the information they can find at schools known for producing graduates who go on to be successful in international business. Others seek the prestige of an American university with a recognized name. Still others wish to develop the English-language skill

International universities are taking advantage of the opportunities to raise their profiles in the Middle East by establishing their own campuses in the region to attract eager students and brilliant researchers from the area. Here, former U.S. president George H.W. Bush and his wife, Barbara Bush, attend the inauguration of the Texas A&M building in Qatar.

and knowledge of Anglophone culture that is increasingly valuable in the international marketplace.

Unfortunately, after the attacks on September 11, 2001, in New York City and Washington D.C., the American government tightened regulations on student visas. It is now more difficult than ever for students to obtain permission to study in this country. Consequently, growing numbers now go to the United Kingdom, Canada, Australia, or universities or institutes that teach in English in other countries. In turn, the government of the UAE is willing to spend money to bring that education to their countries. From many perspectives, this is a win-win-win situation. Students win because they can receive the training they want without traveling around the world. The universities win because they obtain visibility around the world and increase profits. The emirates win because they bring research and development to their countries, and the bright young minds are more likely to remain at home if they can achieve the same goals without going abroad.

As companies around the world shift their focus from national to international markets, they experience a growing need for multilingual graduates who are prepared to deal with people of different cultures, backgrounds, and sensitivities. Because many American universities need the income gained from tuition paid by foreign nationals, they are especially sensitive to the difficulties students experience in getting student visas. Consequently, bringing the university to the Middle East is a helpful compromise. In addition, universities constantly seek to draw skilled researchers who will bring money and prestige to their institutions. Increasing exposure and availability overseas will help them to do that. Furthermore, universities from Europe and other parts of the globe have already established themselves in the country. For example, Dubai Knowledge Village hosts the Dubai branches of Scottish, Australian, Indian, Pakistani, Belgian, Russian, and American universities.

Many American administrators believe that since someone will supply education to the UAE, it might as well be the American institutions that have been so popular with students from abroad. Not only will these programs help benefit the American institutions themselves and the Emirati students, but they may also increase cultural sensitivity and understanding, decreasing future tensions between people of different countries. New York University will offer courses in Abu Dhabi, Michigan State University and the Rochester Institute of Technology will offer courses in Dubai, and George Mason University will offer courses in Ras al-Khaimah.

Despite the enthusiasm of college administrators, American faculty members are slower to embrace the idea of establishing campuses in the Middle East, and without their support, the programs may not be successful. Due to turmoil in that part of the world, not all faculty members are willing to leave the United States for any length of time, especially if they have families they will either have to take with them or leave for several months or a few years. Furthermore, many faculty have become accustomed to great latitude in planning and teaching their courses. Texts that are considered threatening to the traditional values of the area will not necessarily be tolerated, which makes faculty members less than eager to take positions at the new universities.

Another problem that must be resolved before American universities will be successful in attracting Emirati students is the question of granting degrees in the emirates. Some American institutions plan to offer degree-granting programs overseas, but to date, Ivy League schools have refused to do so. While these elite American universities are willing to create educational centers in the UAE, they are not willing to allow students to earn degrees there. In the future, this policy may change, but currently, students who want degrees from Ivy League institutions must come to the United States to earn them.

The increase in the number of universities in the UAE is likely to have a profound impact on society in future years. There will be cultural tension as Western universities establish branches in the UAE. In order for these satellite campuses to succeed, both the universities and the hosts will have to find acceptable compromises if cultural clashes are to be avoided.

8

The Culture of UAE

Since the Louvre was founded in 1793, it has brought to mind images of priceless paintings, sculptures, and antiquities. Many people instantly picture the Mona Lisa or the Venus de Milo when they hear the name of the institution. Built in 1190 as a fortress and serving as a home for members of the French royalty for several hundred years, the museum is now a favorite destination of tourists from all over the world. Soon, however, art lovers from the Middle East will not have to travel to France to see masterpieces of classical European art. In 2007, the Louvre announced its intention to open a branch on Saadiyat Island, just off the coast of Abu Dhabi. A thirty-year agreement between the French Ministry of Culture and Abu Dhabi's Tourism Authority will allow the new branch of the Louvre to display masterpieces from its collection and also from France's other great museums.

Abu Dhabi spent heavily to bring the Louvre to its shores. The museum name and brand cost $525 million, and France received money for a variety of other artistic projects, including an art restoration center. In addition, the original Louvre received funds to cover the renovation of a wing that will house Islamic art. This wing will bear the name of the emirates ruler Sheik Zayed bin Sultan Al Nahyan.

In addition to funds paid to France, the construction of the new building requires financing as well. Designed by French architect Jean Nouvel, the new Louvre will bear a modern design—white, flat and round with a domed roof, and many windows in the roof to allow natural light inside the building. Construction should be completed in 2012.

THE
CULTURAL
DISTRICT

LOUVRE ABU DHABI

In an effort to become a part of the international sphere in a variety of fields, the United Arab Emirates have spent a great deal of money to promote culture, academics, and investments within its borders. A branch of the famous French art museum, the Louvre, for example, will be built in Abu Dhabi and will include artwork from France.

In return for such significant investment, Abu Dhabi will receive a loan of at least 300 works of art for display and experts from the original Louvre to run the museum. In addition to those pieces, the new Louvre will buy works on the authority of a committee of Abu Dhabi's rulers. With the loan of so many works from the Louvre, classical European art will obviously be important, but it will only be one part of the collection. The committee seeks to include all types of art from all parts of the world. Abu Dhabi's tourism board hopes the new Louvre will draw at least 3 million tourists by 2015.

One goal of the new Louvre is to open a dialogue between the East and West about art. But the Louvre will not shoulder this burden alone. Just down the street will be branches of the Guggenheim Museum, a maritime museum, and the projected Sheikh Zayed Museum. These four buildings, combined with a performing arts center, will comprise the new cultural district on Abu Dhabi.

Well-known architect Frank Gehry will design the new branch of the Solomon R. Guggenheim Museum. While the announcement that the Louvre was building a branch in the Middle East surprised many, the news of the latest Guggenheim was not as shocking. This branch joins those in Bilbao, Spain; Venice, Italy; and Berlin, Germany; in addition to those in New York City and Las Vegas in the United States. This new branch, however, will be the largest in the world and will have foreign staff on loan from the Guggenheim Foundation, in addition to Emirati staff members. The collection will include modern art with an emphasis on art original to the Middle East. The Guggenheim Abu Dhabi is set to open in 2011.

The Sheikh Zayed Museum will honor the longtime ruler of the country with its emphasis on regional history. The museum will be divided into galleries that recognize different aspects of the late ruler's life. One gallery will be devoted to the environment. During his lifetime, Sheikh Zayed received recognition from many organizations, including the United Nations and the government of Pakistan, for his dedication to the protection of regional animals and environmentally friendly policies.

Another gallery will illustrate the change undergone by the UAE from being a collection of small tribes into a unified, organized prosperous community with international power. Sheikh Zayed wanted his country to enjoy the wealth earned from the sale of its oil business, and this determination will be shown through the stages of development revealed in the transformation gallery.

The third gallery will show visitors how Sheikh Zayed unified the sometimes-rival emirates into one body with diplomacy and compassion. His ability to create cohesiveness among those with differing viewpoints was crucial in the development of the UAE and that ability will be commemorated in this gallery.

When the country was newly formed, education became a clear goal among those who wanted to improve life for citizens of the UAE. Putting citizens first was also the highest of the ruler's goals. The remaining galleries will show the sheikh's devotion to his people. The sheikh felt that the wealth earned from oil would only be useful to a country whose citizens were prepared to build the country. He also felt that the citizens should benefit from the wealth earned from the sale of oil. The people of the region had lived difficult lives, and the ruler was determined that they should enjoy the benefits of their good fortune. Like the ruler himself, the Sheikh Zayed Museum will bear witness to the many struggles and successes endured by the people of the region in their journey from pre-oil days to the present.

The Maritime Museum, designed by Japanese architect Tadao Ando, will pay homage to the sea's historical and current significance in the region. Located on Saadiyat Island with the Louvre Abu Dhabi, the UAE branch of the Guggenheim, and the Sheikh Zayed Museum, the Maritime Museum will provide visitors with the opportunity to learn much about the country, both past and present.

The Saadiyat Performing Arts Centre will be a venue for music, theater, and dance. It will be designed by Zaha Hadid, a British-Iraqi architect. The center will be home to five theaters devoted to music, opera, and drama. In addition, the building will house a multi-use theater with seating for 6,300 people. In addition, plans may include space for training in the performing arts. The building will complement the new museums on Saadiyat Island and allow visitors to appreciate the natural beauty of the site.

The new museums on the island will be great additions to already existing cultural opportunities in the United Arab Emirates. While the Louvre and the Guggenheim are well-known worldwide, the UAE already boasts several large museums with extensive collections of art and historical objects.

The Al Ain National Museum is one of these. It was established in 1969 by Sheikh Zayed bin Sultan Al Nahyan with an eye toward protecting the region's heritage. The ruler is credited with saying, "A country without a past has neither present nor future." Successful archaeological digs in various locations in Abu Dhabi prompted him to build an institution to preserve that past. Located in the city of Al Ain, the capital of the eastern region of Abu Dhabi, where Sheikh Zayed had been governor before he became the emir of Abu Dhabi in 1966, the museum is run by the Department of Antiquities and Tourism. Located approximately halfway between the Arabian Gulf and the Gulf of Oman, the city has served as a spot for travelers between the two bodies of water for at least 5,000 years, and possibly longer. It's no wonder that Bronze Age and Stone Age artifacts have been found there. Because of its rich regional history and close proximity to the Abu Dhabi International Airport, Al Ain is an ideal spot for this museum.

The Al Ain Museum has two sections, one devoted to archeology, and one devoted to ethnography. The archeology section contains items from the latter part of the Stone Age (5 million years ago to 2500 B.C.) to the Islamic period (A.D.622–1900). Visitors to the archaeology section see tools, crafts, weapons, burial artifacts, maps, coins, and other important archaeological finds. The ethnography section includes information about daily life in the region in the past and present, including childhood, education, government, farming, and fishing. Visitors may see items of clothing, furniture, and jewelry, among other items.

Outside the Al Ain Museum, visitors can see the Sultan Fort. Constructed in approximately 1910, the walls are made from clay and mud bricks, traditional building materials in the region, and the roof is made of palm tree trunks. The fort has rooms for sleeping and cooking, as well as a courtyard and a well that once provided the fort with water. This fort provides an interesting contrast between daily life at the beginning of the last century and today, emphasizing the significant impact of technological and economic changes wrought in the past one hundred years.

With the addition of the Louvre and Guggenheim branches in the United Arab Emirates, the country's existing museums will be able to work more closely with these international organizations to create exciting new exhibits and attractions. The Sharjah Art Museum *(above)* houses an extensive permanent collection, but also features international artists and cooperative exchange exhibitions with other museums.

While the museums on Saadiyat Island and in Al Ain are impressive, the other emirates offer a variety of cultural opportunities to visitors. Sharjah offers visitors the National History Museum, a heritage area, the Sharjah Art Museum that houses an impressive permanent collection, and the Sharjah Art Center where teens and adults may take art classes. The Sharjah Very

Special Arts Museum was founded to improve the lives of the disabled by allowing them a place to learn about, create, and display their art. Dubai's National Museum is located in Al-Fahidi Fort and displays archaeological artifacts and shows how life was lived in Dubai in the past. In nearby Ras al-Khaimah, visitors may visit the Ras al-Khaimah's Archaeological Museum and the Fine Art Association Center, where promising young regional artists' works are displayed.

LITERATURE AND MUSIC

Thanks to satellite television, many Arabic-language programs are available to all Arab countries and to Arabic-speaking viewers around the world. In recent years, one of the most popular programs on UAE television has been *Million's Poet*, which is produced by Abu Dhabi television and attracts over 70 million viewers across the Middle East, Europe, and the United States. What is most interesting, however, is the fact that a television contest would focus on poetry as opposed to singing or dancing competitions. The popularity of this program speaks to the esteem in which poetry is held in Arab countries.

The stage setting and show's production is reminiscent of *American Idol*, a popular show in the United States. On *Million's Poet*, however, the contestants are local poets from the UAE who compose and recite poetry to the audience, and who are judged by professional poets and literature experts. In the first half of the show, the contestants recite poetry of their own composition, according to any topic they choose, but the judges give them a specific topic for the show's second half. The judges then rate the contestants according to the difficulty of their poems, the intricacy of the rhymes, the passion of their delivery, and other criteria. The prize is one million dirhams (about $275,000). Audiences at home also have a chance to affect the selection. The contestants are mostly local Bedouins, who still practice the art of Nabati poetry, which is the native poetry of the Arabian Peninsula. Similar to an ode, Nabati poetry takes various topics as its subjects, including love, heartbreak, loss, and tribal pride. It is recited in the common, local dialect of Arabic, as opposed to classical Arabic, which Arabs write but do not speak, a real problem for modern poets.

Million's Poet is not the only show that takes poetry as its topic. Another popular television program, also produced by Abu Dhabi TV, is *Prince of Poets*. Unlike *Million's Poet*, *Prince of Poet's* competitors compose and recite their verse in classical Arabic and use classical Arabic poetic forms, not Nabati poetry. They also take on social and political issues as the inspiration for their poems.

In the UAE, as well as in other Arab countries, poetry continues to hold an important cultural place in society. Poets play an important role as cultural, social, and political critics. Indeed, many of the contestants on *Million's Poet* and *Prince of Poets* have criticized the U.S.-led invasion of Iraq as well as policies of the local Arab governments toward their own people.

Sheikh Mohammed bin Rashid al-Makhtoum, the vice president of the UAE and prime minister and ruler of Dubai, is a well-known Nabati poet and scholar. He established the Dubai Culture and Arts Authority to essentially promote Dubai as the cultural center of the UAE. Its mission states, "The Authority will develop a world-class arts and cultural infrastructure in Dubai and will promote the visual arts, theatre, music, literature, poetry and various other arts."

The musical tradition of the UAE is just as vibrant as its literary one. Just as Bedouin traditions have colored Nabati poetry, so do they affect and shape the music of the UAE. The music style of the region is known as *khaleeji* music, which is a folk style that uses traditional instruments like the lute, the drums, and the rababa. The word *khaleeji* means "pertaining to the Gulf." In recent years, Western-style music has influenced the UAE scene, and new stars have a Western pop sound. Ahlam is one famous singer who is Bahraini but lives in the UAE; she has recorded a dozen albums, all of which have sold well. Another well-known Emirati singer is Abdel Moneim Saleh, who sings, composes music, and plays the lute. Many music studios operate in the UAE, producing music and supporting both well-known and emerging musicians and performers.

SPORTS

The UAE's citizens enjoy a wide range of sporting and recreational activities. In fact, Dubai is currently building Dubai Sports City, a metropolis with the overwhelming theme of athletics. The future residents of this city in the middle of the desert will live in lush villas amid four stadiums, four athletic academies, and a world-class golf course; people can go shopping and out to eat at the shops and restaurants of the Sports City's sports-themed shopping mall.

Its national pastime is football (which Americans call soccer), a sport that is not native to the UAE's culture. The UAE Football Association (UAE-FA) was established in 1971 and is financially supported by the emirs, so that it now oversees 26 clubs which participate in several competitions such as the Asia Cup and the Arab Cup. The primary football competition in the UAE is the Etisalat National League, which began in 1973. UAE football clubs include al-Shabbab, Al-Jazeera, al-Wahda, al-Wasl, al-Shaab, al-Sharjah, al-Ain, and others. Football receives much support from the UAE's citizens, but also from its leaders. The emirates have built some of the world's most spectacular football stadiums such as Dubai's Al-Maktoum Stadium or Abu Dhabi's Al Nuhayyan Stadium. In 2007, Sheikh Dr. Sultan bin Mohammad al-Qasimi, a member of the UAE Supreme Council and current ruler of Sharjah, gave the Sharjah club players 8 million dirhams for winning the Gulf Cup. After founding football academies in both Ghana and Switzerland, the Brazilian soccer legend Pele has recently proposed his idea to open a Pele Football Academy in the UAE, and he is being courted by the various leaders of the emirates. The academy would help young people between the ages of 5 and 18 to develop and promote their football skills, and also help coach those who want to be professional players. As of this writing, Pele is scouting out the best location in the UAE for his academy.

Car racing—also called car rallying—is another very popular, though non-native sport, in the UAE. It is overseen by the Emirates Motor Sports Federation. Mohammed Ben Sulayem, a popular driver whose career spans more than 20 years, created the UAE Desert Challenge. A six-day racing event that takes place in December, competitors race through the UAE with its varying terrains (including desert, mountains, rocky regions, etc.). The Desert Challenge has been a popular competition since its inception in 1991. Many car rallying events, as well as motorbike races, take place in Dubai's Autodrome.

Another popular Western sport that has been adopted by the UAE is golf. One would think that the desert landscape of the emirates would not be ideal for a sport that requires acres of green playing grounds. However, the Dubai Desert Classic, which is held at the Emirates Golf Club, is currently one of the featured stops on the tour of the Professional Golf Association. Its landscaping is beautiful, with a Bedouin tent theme to remind visitors and competitors that they are in the Middle East.

Some call camel racing, falconry, and boat racing heritage sports because they hearken back to Bedouin tradition. Bedouin used falcons to hunt for food, as falcons were especially adept at capturing small rabbits or other animals, and bringing them back to their owners. The falcons themselves were admired by the Bedouins for their hunting skills and statuesque appearance. In the UAE today, falconry and the raising and training of falcons is a beloved sport that reminds many Emiratis of their Bedouin heritage. Today, trained falcons cost their owners thousands of dollars because of the amount of time and skill required to tame and train the birds. Known as *al qanas*, falconry was also the favorite sport of Sheikh Zayed of Abu Dhabi, who was well known for respecting and enjoying Bedouin traditions. He published a book in 1976, *Hunting with Falcons*, which is considered to be the most important manual on and history of falconry in the region.

Camel racing has become so popular in the United Arab Emirates, there are special camel-racing tracks in the country and even a Camel Reproduction Center in Dubai. The sport's popularity in the Middle East has spread internationally, with some events held in Australia.

Camel racing has its roots as a performance sport, held at special events such as weddings. Recently, the availability of petrodollars and the interest of some of the UAE's leaders have led to the revival of this desert sport, with special tracks such as Nad Al Sheba in Dubai being built especially for these competitions. Other impressive tracks include al Wathba and al Ain tracks in

Abu Dhabi. The training and breeding of the camels is also a big business, as a well-trained camel can cost in the hundreds of thousands of dollars. Races take place between October and March.

In the past, many people in the world criticized the practice of using children as jockeys. In response, the UAE, in conjunction with UNICEF, has taken steps to end the practice of using children in the sport, returning them to their homes and families, providing counseling, health care, and compensation, and outlawing the use of future camel jockeys under the age of 18. The program has been in effect since 2005 and has continued to be successful in finding and assisting young camel jockeys.

Many sporting events in the UAE offer free admission to spectators, a sign of how integral sports is to the culture of the emirates and how much support the events receive from the government.

TELEVISION AND NEWSPAPERS

Many sporting events are broadcast live on television and attract large viewing audiences. Indeed, over the past decade, television has expanded as a result of new satellite technology.

Until the 1990s, most television stations in Arab countries, including the emirates, were owned by the government and heavily censored. However, al-Jazeera, the satellite news station based in Qatar, changed the status quo. Al-Jazeera, though financed by the emir of Qatar, has since it began broadcasting enjoyed a large measure of independence and freedom of the press. It broadcasts news coverage in a professional style, sending reporters all over the Middle East and the world to cover news events. It even places reporters in countries that have traditionally been unfriendly to Arab nations, such as Israel. Al-Jazeera also produces talk and debate programs about news events and current trends, tackling a gamut of political, social, and even religious issues. Al-Jazeera broadcasts via satellite to an Arab-speaking audience across the Middle East and the world.

Within 10 years of al-Jazeera's inception, every major Arab nation had at least one satellite station broadcasting news, politics, and other programs. Specialized channels also developed, covering children's programs, sporting events, and music videos. In the UAE alone, dozens of channels currently exist, including Ajman TV, Abu Dhabi TV, Dubai TV, Abu Dhabi Sports, and many others. UAE residents can also enjoy the ability to view hundreds of channels from around the world in any language, mostly because the population of the emirates is diverse due to the large number of expatriates and foreign workers living there.

In Dubai, plans were formulated in 2001 to build the Dubai Media City (DMC), a media hub in the tiny emirate that allows media-focused businesses to co-exist and work close to one another. One goal is to attract media-based businesses to set up their headquarters there, boasting of its location as a crossroads between Asia, the Middle East, and Africa. It offers first-class media technology, production, and marketing services to help media businesses grow and expand. DMC is an outgrowth of the sheikhs' intentions to diversify their economies. For example, Dubai Media City's Web site states, "DMC is a successful reflection of the vision of His Highness Sheikh Mohammed Bin Rashid Al Maktoum, UAE Vice President, Prime Minister and Ruler of Dubai to transform Dubai into a knowledge-based society and economy."

The growth of newspapers has also mushroomed in the last 20 years. The most popular newspapers include *Al-Ittihad* and *Al-Khaleej*, but many others exist as well, catering to various interests. Some newspapers cover general news and politics, such as *7 Days*, *Al-Ittihad*, and *Gulf Today*, while others have a business and financial focus, such as *Gulf News*. Many newspapers are also available in English, such as *Gulf News*, *Khaleej Times*, and others, and have a substantial online presence. Reporting by UAE journalists is generally of high quality and very professional. Many reporters come from other Arab countries, or even from Western news agencies, recruited by UAE media to do an outstanding job. While some people believe the government censors journalists, most journalists, readers, and viewers believe the press enjoy more freedom in the UAE than in other Arab countries.

9

The Future of UAE

Historically, commerce has always been an important activity in the UAE, where merchants over the centuries made their living in trading with China, India, and the Spice Islands (present-day Indonesia). It has only grown more important in recent years. For centuries, people have met at the *souk*, or market, not only to shop, but also to socialize. The souk has always been a place to buy food or other household items, and now the selection is even larger than in the past. Furthermore, it is still possible to bargain, allowing people to buy things at extremely reasonable prices, provided consumers know how to haggle. The selection of items for sale has grown from an assortment of daily necessities to include luxury clothing, electronics, and expensive jewelry.

Recently, the UAE has built many huge shopping malls for a variety of reasons. First, Dubai hopes to compete with Hong Kong in drawing tourists around the world seeking an upscale shopping experience. Second, it is entirely too hot during the summer months for people to gather outside, and with many children and teens on breaks from school, the mall provides a safe, comfortable place where mothers and their children can gather and socialize with others. Third, malls allow women to socialize without fear of encountering difficult social situations. Traditionally, it has been considered inappropriate for a woman to publicly speak to a man who is not her husband or relative. Since some malls do not permit young men to enter during specified hours, the women can roam freely through the mall to shop or chat with friends. In some malls, young men are not

Ski Dubai, located in the Mall of the Emirates, is the first indoor ski resort in the Middle East. Featuring five ski runs from beginner to advanced, Ski Dubai fills the area with enough snow to fill about three football fields.

allowed in certain areas, in keeping with regional and religious traditions.

Many of the large malls are located in Dubai, known as the shopping capital of the Middle East. The Mall of the Emirates, for example, contains many upscale shops such as Swedish clothing store H&M and the American department store Saks Fifth Avenue. Major designers such as Ralph Lauren and Yves St.

Laurent are represented, as are a plethora of specialty stores and outlets. Shoppers can eat at a variety of restaurants or in one of two food courts. In addition to all of the shopping and dining establishments, this mall boasts Ski Dubai, a winter-themed park that includes a ski slope, tobogganing, and play areas. The mall also features Magic Planet, an amusement park with rides and games. When people are tired from shopping, skiing, and playing, they can take in a film at a luxury movie theater. Shoppers can do everything from exchange currency at one of the banks in the mall to recharge their mobile phones at a recharging station. Furthermore, in order to draw tourists, the mall is attached to a large luxury hotel with childcare, a spa, fitness center, and swimming pool.

The Mall of the Emirates is the largest shopping mall in the Middle East, but it may soon lose that distinction to the Mall of Arabia or the Dubai Mall. The Mall of Arabia will be part of the City of Arabia inside the Dubailand theme park. When completed, Dubailand will be 3 billion square feet in size, twice as large as Walt Disney World in Florida. Its planners hope it will attract tourists of all ages, backgrounds, and nationalities. Scheduled to open in 2010, the park will be divided into six "worlds" with different themes, including attractions, sports, the environment, relaxation, shopping, and entertainment. Like the Mall of the Emirates, the City of Arabia will host many shops, boutiques, and restaurants. The mall is planned to divide the normally bustling, louder areas, such as those where families with children might shop, from those where people might seek calm, such as the spa and stores selling luxury goods. In addition, the mall will have a bowling alley and a performance stage, and serve as the entrance to the dinosaur theme park.

The Dubai Mall, like the Mall of Arabia and the Mall of the Emirates, will contain an enormous collection of luxury stores and restaurants. In addition, the Dubai Mall will include Atlantis, an aquatic attraction and one of the world's largest aquarium, an ice skating rink, and a gold souk where visitors may find an impressive array of jewels and gold.

Shopping is quite popular among the citizens and expatriates who live in the UAE. In addition to the numerous malls and souks, shopping festivals are held to attract even more shoppers. People receive large discounts on merchandise and enjoy entertainment, fireworks, raffles, and prizes. These festivals attract not just local shoppers but also shoppers from abroad who enjoy not just the shopping but also the experience of staying in the UAE. These new malls and festivals will draw tourists, businesses, and money to the area. While petroleum funds may be declining, funds from tourists, especially those shoppers enjoying the "national pastime" of shopping will be growing quickly.

THE PALM ISLANDS

The world's largest artificial islands, The Palm Islands, have been called the Eighth Wonder of the World. They are truly impressive modern engineering achievements. When the project is complete, the three islands will add a total of 323 miles (520 kilometers) of shoreline to the country's existing beaches, increase tourism revenue, and provide a luxurious haven for tourists seeking unusual attractions in a unique setting.

While many are impressed by the structure of the Palm Islands, not everyone knows why they were built in their unusual shape. Tourism in Dubai has been increasing since the mid-1990s. Nevertheless, by 2000, the country was running out of beachfront property. In response to this problem, Dubai's ruler, Sheikh Mohammed bin Rashid Al Maktoum, imagined man-made islands shaped like palm trees that would increase the amount of shoreline in Dubai and draw tourists and residents alike. The sheikh's plan provided far more beachfront property than round islands could supply. The fact that the islands can be seen from the air by approaching visitors, and even from space, simply adds to their appeal.

Each island is shaped like a palm tree nearly surrounded by a crescent. Why did the builders choose palm trees? The date palm is significant in this part of the world. Native to the region, the tree has long been a source of food, and dates have been a staple in the Arabian Middle Eastern diet since ancient times. Furthermore, date palms usually grow near water, making them a welcome sight to someone who has been traveling through a desert. The crescent-shaped part of the island surrounds each palm tree, serves as a breakwater, and protects the trunk and fronds of the tree from harsh weather and the resulting erosion.

CREATING THE PALM ISLANDS

Before the Sheikh's vision could be implemented, experts studied all aspects of the project to ensure that marine and plant life would remain unharmed. Because many tourists are expected to visit the islands to see fish and plant life native to the Middle East, efforts were made to design and build the islands without destroying the natural environment. In addition, those involved with the project hoped to improve the natural environment, increasing the number of species of plants, animals, and fish living in the area. While the islands could have been built less expensively and more quickly with traditional construction materials such as metal, the environment might have suffered. For these reasons, only natural materials were used to create the islands.

Since the islands are artificial, great care had to be taken to protect them from erosion and the rough storms that can arise in the Persian Gulf. A smaller version of the breakwater was created and tested extensively in a variety of weather conditions to make certain the structure could not only survive rough weather but also protect the fronds and trunk of the tree.

Once the project was deemed feasible, plans were made to build the islands. Before the trunk and fronds of the palm could be created, the 6.8-mile-long crescent had to be constructed to protect the rest of the project as it was being built. Rocks were taken from quarries in Dubai and placed using a Differential Global Position System (DGPS). Engineers and divers coordinated their efforts to ensure that the rocks were put in exactly the right places, starting on the floor of the Gulf and rising to about 14 feet above sea level. Consequently, the crescent can survive waves of up to about 13 feet. Furthermore, to protect the quality of the water inside the crescent, each breakwater has two gaps to allow water to flow freely into and out of the Gulf.

When the crescents were finished, the trunks and fronds themselves could be constructed through a process called land reclamation. When land is "reclaimed" in this method, sand, rock, and other materials are literally piled high from the ocean floor to high above sea level. Developers throughout the world had already successfully used this method to increase the size of beaches and create islands, but this project was far more sophisticated than any previously attempted. First, sand and rock were dredged, or gathered, from the bottom of the Persian Gulf and sprayed into place. Because the spray of sand resembles an arch, the process is sometimes called rainbowing. A Global Positioning System, or GPS, is used to make sure the land is placed correctly. Once the land is in place, machines compact it until it is very dense and able to support the weight of the buildings planned for it. The process was so effective in the creation of the Palm Jumeirah that the land on the island is actually more dense than the mainland.

THE PALM JUMEIRAH

The Palm Jumeirah, the first of the islands, measures 3 miles by 3 miles. This island is named after the Jumeirah region of Dubai where residents traditionally earned their living from pearl diving and fishing. Today, however, Jumeirah boasts a wealthier clientele than it has had in the past.

Building commenced in 2001, and the first residents moved to the island in 2007. The trunk is filled with luxury apartments and hotels as well as places to shop and dine. Eventually, the Golden Mile, a strip of land on the trunk, will contain a variety

The United Arab Emirates' wealth has given its citizens and foreign residents opportunities to enjoy a more luxurious side of life. Here, a man enjoys the view from the balcony of his home on one of the Palm Islands.

of beautiful waterfront homes and businesses. When finished, the region's first monorail will transport people from the bottom of the trunk to the crescent and points between. The fronds are the site of many villas and waterfront townhomes.

World-renowned businesses like the Trump Organization have already begun building on the Palm Jumeirah. The Trump International Hotel and Tower, projected to be complete in 2009, will provide luxurious hotel and residence space. Another luxury hotel, The Atlantis, owned by Kerzner International, located on the crescent, will provide not only an enormous, ocean-themed luxury hotel, but also a water park and the largest outdoor marine habitat in the Middle East.

THE PALM JEBEL ALI

The Palm Jebel Ali will measure 4.6 miles by 4.6 miles when finished. Construction began in 2002 and, as of this writing, should be completed in 2008. While the Palm Jumeirah contains many residences and hotels, the Palm Jebel Ali is designed to draw those seeking entertainment. This island, much larger than its predecessor, has room for such entertainment areas as a large theme park and several marinas, as well as other types of entertainment for both adults and children.

THE PALM DEIRA

At 10.5 miles by 5.5 miles, the Palm Deira is the largest of the three islands. The developer, Al Nakheel Properties, envisions a city of more than one million people on the complex when the project is complete. In addition to a massive land reclamation effort larger than the one undertaken in the construction of either the Palm Jumeirah or the Palm Jebel Ali, construction of this island will involve modifications to Dubai Creek, one of the country's most important waterways.

THE WORLD

In 2003, the ruler of Dubai announced plans for his next endeavor, The World. This group of 300 islands, also visible from space, looks like a map of the world surrounded by an oval breakwater. Measuring nearly 5.5 miles in length and 3.7 miles in width with an average of 328 feet between each island, the development adds approximately 144 miles of beachfront property to the country's coastline. Accessible only by air and water, The World will attract attracts those looking for privacy as well as luxury homes, resorts, and communities.

From the Pirate Coast to The World, the emirates' history in the past 200 years has been startling in terms of change. Having evolved from a small pirate coast where 19th-century seamen feared for their lives and for the security of their cargoes to a haven of elites, upscale shopping, and high culture, the UAE will, assuming political stability, surely continue to grow and strengthen its unique, position as one of the Middle East's and the world's most innovative and yet deeply traditional places.

Chronology

1820 The British government and leaders of six of the Arabian coastal sheikhdoms sign a treaty in hopes of decreasing piracy crime in the area.

1892 The emirates agree that they will control domestic affairs while Great Britain will have control of external matters.

1952 The seven emirates form the Trucial Council.

1955 A border dispute between Saudi Arabia and Abu Dhabi results in occupation of Buraimi by the Trucial Oman Levees, Arab forces led by British officers.

1958 Oil is discovered in Abu Dhabi.

1966 Sheikh Zayed bin Sultan al Nahyan assumes control of Abu Dhabi, and several members of the ruling family take administrative positions in the government.

1968 Great Britain announces its plan to withdraw all forces from the emirates by the end of 1971. The announcement leads to interest in a federation of the emirates.

1970 Iran claims three islands and eventually acquires control of them: Greater and Lesser Tunbs, and Abu Musa.

1971 Great Britain and the emirates sign a treaty of friendship. Sheikh Zayed bin Sultan al Nahyan guides the emirates in the formation of the federation. He is elected president, and his vice president is Sheikh Rashid bin Saeed al Maktoum. The alliance's goals include education of citizens, peaceful conflict resolution in the area, reinforcement of connections in the region, and involvement in global coalitions.

1973 The oil departments of Abu Dhabi, Dubai, and Sharjah are consolidated. The 1973 oil crisis begins on October 17, 1973, and eventually ends March 17, 1974 when oil ministers announce the end of the embargo against the United States.

1974   Sheikh Zayed allots significant funding to growing countries as well as other Arabic and Islamic states.

1981   Bahrain, Kuwait, Oman, Qatar, Saudi Arabia, and the UAE join to create the Gulf Cooperation Council, an organization with the goal of working together on a variety of projects.

1983   The Abu Dhabi Women's Association moves to new headquarters, and Sheikh Zayed says that although Islam gives women the role of raising children, women are not limited to childrearing.

1985   On National Day, Sheikh Zayed declares his belief that people are the main asset of the UAE and that the primary objective of the federation is to serve the people, affirming his commitment to the citizens.

Timeline

1971
Great Britain and the emirates sign a treaty of friendship. Sheikh Zayed bin Sultan al Nahyan of Abu Dhabi helps establish the United Arab Emirates

1820
The British government signs an agreement with Trucial sheikhs to stop piracy in the Gulf

1958
Oil is discovered in Abu Dhabi

1820   1971

1968
Great Britain announces it will withdraw all forces from the emirates by the end of 1971

1892
Another agreement with the British government gives England the right to control the external affairs of the Trucial states

1989 Sheikh Zayed speaks in favor of the possibility of stable relations with the Soviet Union.

1990 Iraq invades Kuwait, and the UAE criticizes the action and joins the coalition against Saddam Hussein.

1991 The UAE makes it clear that although assistance from friendly countries is welcome, permanent foreign military bases are not.

1995 Sheikh Zayed calls for an end to UN sanctions against Iraq, saying that Iraqis, rather than Saddam Hussein himself, were suffering because of the embargo.

1996 The constitution of the UAE becomes permanent, and Abu Dhabi becomes the capital.

1997 Because of the lack of progress in peace talks and lack of support from other Arab leaders, the UAE refuses

1973–1974
Arab oil-producing countries place an embargo on the United States and other Western nations for their support of Israel

1981
Bahrain, Kuwait, Oman, Qatar, Saudi Arabia, and the UAE join to create the Gulf Cooperation Council

1973   2004

1991
The UAE states that permanent foreign military bases are not welcome in their countries

1996
The constitution of the UAE becomes permanent, and Abu Dhabi becomes the capital of the UAE

2004
Sheikh Zayed, the UAE's first president, dies

to participate in the Middle East and North Africa economic meeting.

1998 The UAE restores diplomatic ties with Iraq.

1999 The ruler of Oman, His Majesty Sultan Qaboos, and Sheikh Zayed sign an agreement to prevent border disputes between the UAE and Oman.

The UAE criticizes the re-establishment of diplomatic relations between Saudi Arabia and Iran. Thanks to Qatar, positive relations are restored.

2001 Sheikh Zayed confirms UAE support for Palestinian National Authority policy regarding Israeli hostility.

2004 The first woman minister in the UAE, Sheikha Lubna Al Qasimi, is appointed to the Cabinet.

Sheikh Zayed dies. His son, General Sheikh Mohammed bin Zayed al Nahyan becomes Crown Prince of Abu Dhabi.

2005 General Sheikh Mohammed bin Zayed al Nahyan becomes Deputy Supreme Commander of the UAE military, including army, navy, and air forces.

2006 Sheikh Maktoum bin Rashid al Maktoum dies, his brother, His Highness Sheikh Mohammed bin Rashid al Maktoum becomes the ruler of Dubai and vice-president of the UAE.

"About Dubai Knowledge Village," Dubai Knowledge Village 2004. Available online at http://kv.ae/en/.

"About Zayed University," Zayed University. Available online at http://www.zu.ac.ae/html/aboutzu.html.

Al Jandaly, Bassma. "Sharjah's decency law takes effect today," *Gulf News*. Available online at http://archive.gulfnews.com/articles/01/09/26/27418.html.

"Bush, Congress Clash Over Port Sale," CNN.com. Available online at http://www.cnn.com/2006/POLITICS/02/21/port.security/.

"Culture of United Arab Emirates," Countries and Their Cultures 2007. Thomson Corporation. Available online at http://www.everyculture.com/To-Z/United-Arab-Emirates.html.

"Country Study: UAE," Library of Congress. Available online at http://lcweb2.loc.gov/cgi-bin/query/r?frd/cstdy:@field(DOCID+ae0078).

"Centre of Excellence for Applied Research and Training," Higher Colleges of Technology—HCT United Arab Emirates. Available online at http://www.hct.ac.ae/cert/aspx/cert.aspx.

"General Authority of Islamic Affairs & Endowment," Abu Dhabi Government. Available online at http://www.abudhabi.ae/Sites/Portal/Citizen/EN/departments,did=14956.html#overview.

"HCT at a Glance," Higher Colleges of Technology. HCT United Arab Emirates. Available online at http://www.hct.ac.ae/misc/aspx/hct_at_a_glance.aspx?p=aa.

Hardy, Roger. "Analysis: Inside Wahhabi Islam." BBC News. Available online at http://news.bbc.co.uk/2/hi/middle_east/1571144.stm.

Hawley, Donald. *The Trucial States*. New York: Twayne Publishers, 1970.

"History of Al Ain National Museum," Al Ain National Museum Department of Antiquities and Tourism. Available online at http://www.aam.gov.ae/history/index.htm.

"House Panel Votes to Block Port Deal," FOX News. Available online at http://www.foxnews.com/story/0,2933,187147,00.html.

"Information about al-Fujayrah." Available online at http://en.wikipedia.org/wiki/Fujairah.

"Information for Visitors," The National Museum of Ras al-Khaimah. Available online at http://www.rakmuseum.gov.ae/.

"Interactive Map," Dubailand 2007. Available online at http://www.dubailand.ae/#.

Karam, P. Andrew. "Oil Is Discovered in the Middle East". Available online at http://www.bookrags.com/research/oil-is-discovered-in-the-middle-eas-scit-061/.

Killgore, Andrew I. "In Memoriam: Sheikh Zayed bin Sultan Al Nahyan (1918–2004)," Washington Report on Middle East Affairs, March 2005. Available online at http://www.wrmea.com/archives/March_2005/0503041.html.

Lewin, Tamar. "U.S. Universities Rush to Set Up Outposts Abroad," New York Times. Available online at http://www.nytimes.com/2008/02/10/education/10global.html?_r=2&oref=slogin&pagewanted=print.

Roger Louis, William. Ends of British Imperialism: The Scramble for Empire, Suez, and Decolonization. New York: IB Tauris Books, 2006.

"Louvre Museum to Build Branch in UAE," USA Today. Available online at http://www.usatoday.com/news/world/2007-03-06-louvre-abu-dhabi_N.htm.

Maadad, Sana, and Meraj Rizvi. "Federal Law on Marriages Likely to Be Unveiled Soon," Khaleej Times. Available online at http://www.khaleejtimes.com/Displayarticle.asp?section=theuae&xfile=data/theuae/2003/september/theuae_september301.xml.

"Mall of the Emirates." Available online at http://www.malloftheemirates.com/default.asp.

"Minister Highlights Government's Efforts to Empower Emirati Women," UAE Interact. Emirates News Agency. Available online at http://uaeinteract.com/docs/Minister_highlights_governments_efforts_to_empower_Emirati_women/24320.htm.

Mussallam, Nada S. "What's Rocking the Marriages in the UAE," *Khaleej Times*. Available online at http://www.khaleejtimes.com/DisplayArticleNew.asp?section=theuae&xfile=data/theuae/2007/november/theuae_november516.xml.

"Overview," *City of Arabia*. Mall of Arabia. Available online at http://www.cityofarabia.ae/mall_of_arabia.htm.

"Progress on the Guggenheim Abu Dhabi," The Solomon R. Guggenheim Foundation. Available online at http://www.guggenheim.org/news/index.html.

Robson, Victoria. "Interview with Sheikha Lubna Al-Qasimi, UAE Economy Minister," *MEED*. Available online at http://www.meed.com/economy/features/2008/01/interview_with_sheikha_lubna_alqasimi_uae_economy_minister.html.

"Sharjah, United Arab Emirates 2002," Sharjah Commerce and Tourism Development Authority. Available online at http://www.sharjah-welcome.com/index.php.

"Sheikh Zayed Museum Planned," *AME Info*. Available online at http://www.ameinfo.com/121285.html.

Siddiqi, Asif. "The Beginnings of British Commercial Aviation." U.S. Centennial of Flight Commission Web site. Available online at http://www.centennialofflight.gov/essay/Commercial_Aviation/britain/Tran18.htm.

"Survey Reveals 46pc Divorce Rate in UAE," *Khaleej Times*. Available online at http://www.khaleejtimes.com/DisplayArticleNew.asp?section=theuae&xfile=data/theuae/2005/september/theuae_september502.xml.

"The Dubai Mall." *Burj Dubai*. Emaar Properties. Available online at http://www.thedubaimall.com/.

"The UAE Women's Federation," *ArabNet*. Available online at http://www.arab.net/uae/ue_womenfederation.htm.

"UAE Timeline," Emirates.org. 2006–2007. Available online at http://www.emirates.org/timeline.html.

"2007 Report on International Religious Freedom," United States Bureau of Democracy, Human Rights and Labor; "United Arab Emirates," U.S. Department of State, The Office of Electronic

Information, Bureau of Public Affairs, Washington. Available online at http://www.state.gov/g/drl/rls/irf/2007/90223.htm.

Wheeler, Julia. "Obituary: Sheikh Zayed," BBC. Available online at http://news.bbc.co.uk/2/hi/middle_east/3975849.stm.

"Women in the UAE," UAE Federal E-government Portal–UAE Federal Government. Available online at http://www.uae.gov.ae/Government/women.htm#Maternity%20Leave.

"Women in the UAE: Employment," *ArabNet*. Available online at http://www.arab.net/uae/ue_womenemploy.htm.

Further Resources

Cottrell, Alvin J., ed. *The Persian Gulf States*. Baltimore: Johns Hopkins University Press, 1980.

Editors of Time Out. *Time Out Dubai: Abu Dhabi and the UAE*. New York: Time Out Guides, 2007.

Federal Research Division. *United Arab Emirates: A Country Study*. Whitefish, Mont.: Kessinger Publishing, 2004.

Johnson, Julia. *United Arab Emirates*. New York: Chelsea House, 2000.

Dunston, Lara and Terry Carter. *Lonely Planet Dubai Encounter*. New York: Lonely Planet Publications, 2007.

Miller, Debra A. *Modern Nations of the World–United Arab Emirates*. Farmington Hills, Mich.: Lucent Books, 2004.

Rugh, Andrea B. *The Political Culture of Leadership in the United Arab Emirates*. New York: Palgrave Macmillan, 2007.

Sonneborn, Liz. *United Arab Emirates: Enchantment of the World*. Danbury, Conn.: Franklin Watts, 2008.

Wheeler, Julia and Paul Thuysbaert. *Telling Tales: An Oral History of Dubai*. Dubai, United Arab Emirates: Explorer Publishing, 2005.

Web sites

AME Info—Middle East business and financial news
http://www.ameinfo.com/united_arab_emirates/

CIA-The World Factbook—Comprehensive geographic information for every country and territory in the world
https://www.cia.gov/library/publications/the-world-factbook/geos/ae.html

Embassy of the United States, Abu Dhabi, UAE
http://abudhabi.usembassy.gov/

Gulf News—Online edition of Gulf News newspaper

http://www.gulfnews.com/aboutus/gulfnews/index.html

UAE Interact—News and information on the United Arab Emirates

http://uaeinteract.com/

United Arab Emirates Newspapers

http://www.onlinenewspapers.com/une.htm

Picture Credits

Index

About the Contributors

Author **Susan Muaddi Darraj** is associate professor of English at Harford Community College in Bel Air, Maryland. Her book, *Scheherazade's Legacy: Arab and Arab American Women on Writing*, was published in 2004. Her short story collection, *The Inheritance of Exile*, was published in 2007 by University of Notre Dame Press. She is senior editor of *The Baltimore Review*.

Author **Meredyth Puller** is assistant professor of English at Harford Community College in Bel Air, Maryland. She teaches research writing, literature, and creative writing. She is also a fiction editor for *The Baltimore Review*.

Series editor **Arthur Goldschmidt Jr.** is a retired professor of Middle East History at Penn State University. He has a B.A. in economics from Colby College and his M.A. and Ph.D. degrees from Harvard University in history and Middle Eastern Studies. He is the author of *A Concise History of the Middle East*, which has gone through eight editions, and many books, chapters, and articles about Egypt and other Middle Eastern countries. His most recent publication is *A Brief History of Egypt*, published by Facts on File in 2008. He lives in State College, PA, with his wife, Louise. They have two grown sons.